The Meatball Cookbook

Jez Felwick is

The Bowler, delivering gourmet
meatballs, fish balls, and veg balls from The Lawn
Ranger ,his grass-fed, van to various locations around the
UK. All balled by hand, his Great Balls of Fire have garnered
fans (or ballers) from food critics to fashionistas. Jez learned to
cook at the organic farm and cooking school, Ballymaloe, near Cork
in the Republic of Ireland, before discovering the "food truck" scene on
a trip to the U.S., which inspired the launch of The Bowler.

Currently a regular on the London street food scene,
The Bowler also makes appearances at farmers' markets,
music events, and summer festivals throughout the UK.
Find him on Twitter @TheBowlerUK, or online at
thebowleruk.tumblr.com.

The Meatball Cookbook

Jez Felwick

Mitchell Beazley

For Mum and Dad,
with much love.

First published in Great Britain in 2013
by Mitchell Beazley,
an imprint of Octopus Publishing Group Ltd.,
Endeavour House, 189 Shaftesbury Avenue,
London WC2H 8JY UK
www.octopusbooks.co.uk

A Hachette UK Company
www.hachette.co.uk

Distributed in the U.S. by Hachette Book Group USA
237 Park Avenue, New York NY 10017
www.octopusbooksusa.com

Distributed in Canada by Canadian Manda Group
165 Dufferin Street, Toronto, Ontario, Canada M6K 3H6

Publisher Alison Starling
Senior editor Sybella Stephens
Art direction and design Juliette Norsworthy
Illustrator Abigail Read
Photography Cristian Barnett
Home economist Annie Rigg
Recipe tester Catherine Phipps
Prop stylist Liz Belton
Production Lucy Carter

ISBN: 978 1 84533 763 6

Printed and bound in China

Medium-sized eggs and whole milk should be
used, unless otherwise stated.

Contents

Let's get the ball rolling …

I feel privileged to have been given the opportunity to write this book at such an exciting time for the street food scene. It's been a year since I launched The Bowler. A year-long white-knuckle ride of big-dipping decisions, drops into the unknown, and feeling the rush of serving people food I've created. Not to mention getting to grips with a whole host of regulations, legalities, financial fun times, and new media. The side orders have involved dealing with the nerves, the stress, juggling my personal life, together with the sweat, tiredness, and backache that come with the territory.

I was lucky to grow up surrounded and exposed to all sorts of food by a family who loved to cook, eat, and entertain. Grandmothers from Devon and the East End of London who produced the best pasties and roasts, a mom with understated skills in the kitchen who can turn her hand to anything, as long as her trusty kitchen timers are nearby. Dad left the air force and worked his way up the food chain, becoming a very successful grocer. I used to eat everything, until my little brother Matt came along, I'm told, but after a few years on attention-seeking hunger strikes, I got back on the gravy train and have been eating ever since.

The Bowler wasn't a totally planned initiative, nor was it totally random. Several years back, I decided to have a four-month sabbatical from work and used the inheritance money my GM (grandma) had left me to go to Ballymaloe, a cooking school set on an organic farm near Cork in Ireland. The three months I spent there changed everything. Cooking gave me time to relax and provided me with a quiet time to focus, away from other distractions. I returned to London and looked for a way I could get involved with the farmers' market scene, which had been brought to my attention in Ireland. I hooked up with a Hertfordshire-based organic chicken and egg farmer, as I wanted to get hold of lots of chicken carcasses in order to make fresh stock for organic soup. I started working for the farmer, dropping off produce to be sold at various locations in London and then running the market stand in Clapham (southwest London). Not only did I get an insight into how the farm was run, but it was a quick way to sell pots of homemade soup at various markets. As a weekend job this gave me an outlet to practice some of the things I'd learned in Ireland. I ran the stands and sold soup for many months before the real job, and life, distracted me again.

Cooking and the food business kept niggling at me, though. Then the "food truck" scene in the U.S. caught my attention. Amazing trucks selling the most delicious and varied food. I read, researched, and took to the kitchen. I thought this could be the way to get into the marketplace without spending thousands in investment. When I was first thinking about the food I wanted to sell, I knew I wanted something that was easy to "get." Something that didn't need an explanation. Something that could have maximum flavor within it, but also within the sauce it came in. Then, kapow! I was hit straight on. Not by a ball, but by a thought. Meatballs.

Everyone loves a meatball: the flavor combinations and possibilities are endless, they're fun, they're comforting, they conjure up all sorts of nostalgic childhood memories because people have grown up eating them, and almost every culture has its own variation—albóndigas, frikadelle, köttbullar, kofte, polpette, to name but a few. Meatballs and recipes using ground meat are mentioned in the Roman cooking text *Apicius*, where it says that ground peacock is the best meat to use, followed by pheasant. (My favorite peacock recipe will be in book two.)

The obsession began. I started grinding my own meat in search of the perfect ball, and entered London's emerging street food scene, as this was a reasonably affordable way to get to sell my food and get feedback. What started out as a weekend passion-project-hobby-cum-trial really began to gain momentum. I was offered a spot to trade at a two-day music festival on Clapham Common, in London. Page 1 of the catering handbook says: "Don't trade at a 15,000-people-a-day festival for your first event." However, Andy Ashton, the show's manager, was very persuasive: "Look. It's a great opportunity to see what it's like trading at a festival with a really nice team of people, before you head out into the real world that's full of grouchy so and so's." Fair point. I went looking for more "No, don't be stupids" from Robin Bidgood of Smart Hospitality, a top London caterer. "Sounds like a great idea. It would be a good test. We can help you, I'm sure." Not the answer I was looking for. Finally, as I tried to frame it as a risky and bad idea, Petra Barran of UK street food collective Eat.St merely said, "Why wouldn't you do it?" I had effectively given myself an enormous challenge to undertake single-handed, with a little help from my friends. Four days of little or no sleep ensued. It was exhilarating.

I was chomping at the bit to get a van of some sort when the Lawn Ranger galloped straight onto eBay. Perfect. Well, sort of. Page 2 of the catering handbook says, "Get a vehicle that is suited to your operation." Not quite the case with the Lawn Ranger, but he's definitely a head-turner, and before long I was invited to be part of the massive Friday night street market, The Long Table, in Dalston, London, where 2,000 people turned up at a 500-capacity parking lot filled with a few food traders and a bar.

Food fanatic Twitter lovers started congregating @tweat_up's, and before long I was invited to feed the already full at the UK Chilli Stand Off, followed by a regular spot at the inaugural Brockley Market in southeast London. On each occasion I was honored to attend, felt proud to be there, and would always meet such great and positive people. The food streets aren't lined with gold, but the people you meet and the experiences are, which is why it is such a great thing to be involved with. I have met some amazing new people, all committed to the same cause, and driven by similar passions. We've laughed along the way and been fed, well fed, on all levels.

It's taken me a while to get here, but there's nothing wrong with that. Sometimes things niggle away at us. It's hard to take that first step, to break the routine, to throw yourself into something new. Food had been that niggle. In fact, nibble might be more appropriate. Nibbling away, but being fed by the fear that doing something totally different would be foolish.

This book contains some of my favorite ball recipes to date. Balls that I have taken on the road, sold at the markets, as well as cooked at home. It provides you with ball skills to enable you to adapt and create your own succulent spheres. But merely the fact that I have had the opportunity to write this shows anyone who is teetering on the brink of making a decision to jump into something new that it can only be a good thing. You may not make a mint at whatever it is you choose to do, but the experience you will have and people you meet will be priceless.

Life's about putting your balls on the line once in a while, but in the meantime read, roll, sauce, side, salad, and support your local street food entrepreneurs.

It's all about the meat

The problem with many ready-made meatballs is that they simply don't tell you exactly what cuts of meat they are made from. I also have a slight trust issue generally when it comes to ground meat. I've found that buying cheaper cuts of meat and ready-ground meat from supermarkets yields different results. Ready-ground meat will result in a tasty meatball, but you may notice a lot of liquid and fat leaks out, and that they shrink. This could be down to a number of factors, but I have found that it doesn't happen with whole cuts of meat I have ground myself or bought from my butcher.

It was important for me to buy a variety of cuts of meat and actually grind them myself, but living in a one-bedroom apartment in London didn't lend itself to storing vast amounts of equipment. Luckily my mom, Lynne, is a hoarder par excellence. A quick call to her and off I went to pick up her grinder. It turned out she'd bought it at a swap meet decades ago for $3.18 (about $5), according to the price tag. It was better looking, in a retro way, than it was practical, but it chewed its way though the first few pork shoulders and pieces of beef chuck I threw at it. Then I discovered a handy meat-grinding attachment for my KitchenAid and I was away.

I know that it may not be practical to grind your own meat, so I would urge you to get to know a butcher who will do it for you. Of course, every cookbook you read tells you to do this, but that's because it really is the best thing to do. Say you want to make the best meatballs in the world—that will trigger a conversation where he gives you his opinion, and you're off.

You have the beginnings of a relationship where you can bond over meat. I ask for the meat to be put through the machine twice to distribute the fat more evenly.

Provenance is key. Free-range and organic butchers should be able to trace each beast back to the field. Your butcher should know most about the quality, welfare, and condition of the meat he gets, and where it's from. I was at my butcher's recently when I overheard him ending a relationship with a high-quality pork producer because he had noticed that the fat content of the animals had been diminishing, signs that there could have been changes in their diet, age, and welfare. It was a shame, as the supplier was just down the road, but quality is quality. It was reassuring to witness this. All good butchers will have this level of commitment to the product they buy and sell. I believe it is better to pay a little more in order to make sure that farmers are able to produce the best meat, in the best conditions, at a fair price for them, rather than being squeezed by the demands of having to produce a vast quantity at the lowest price.

Good meat shouldn't smell and it certainly shouldn't be discolored or slimy. The best meats for meatballs are often not the most expensive cuts either. All the more reason that the meat you use should be the best. Meatballs do, by their nature, lend themselves to making a smaller amount of meat go a long way. I've found the best cuts for making meatballs include pork and lamb shoulder as well as beef chuck. These cuts are full of flavor and have a good level of both meat and fat.

Meatball basics

Meatballs are almost impossible to mess up. If you are using the best ingredients to start with, at worst, you will end up with a super-tasty meat sauce in the unlikely event that your balls disintegrate. After much research and experimentation into the elements that make up a great ball, I have identified some basic balling techniques that can be applied (although there is by no means a right or wrong here, so do experiment):

I use breadcrumbs in most of my recipes. Japanese panko breadcrumbs, in particular, are dry, so they absorb the moisture and fat in meatballs, helping to stop the balls from drying out, but they are also fairly rough, which gives the balls a rustic texture. I like this—I'm not a fan of balls that seem overprocessed and smooth. For smaller numbers at home I will cut the crusts off of some 1–2-day-old bread and blitz it in a food processor to get a fine crumb. The crumbs can be stored in an airtight container for up to a month.

Tearing bread and soaking it is a method championed by many and is a good idea if you think your ingredients could benefit from added moisture, and this method helps add a certain lightness.

Store-bought natural crumbs are another alternative. Heading into the more left-field carbohydrates, crushed crackers, oats, and rice will all help absorb moisture, retaining the flavor in the ball, as well as adding texture. I would stay away from anything that already has seasoning in it, because you want to be able to control that yourself.

Combinations of meat can be great to experiment with. Mixing pork with beef, with veal, with chicken, and with shrimp can be interesting. Throwing cured meats, such as Serrano ham, bacon, or chorizo into the mix leads to great results. If you want to use a lean meat like venison, try adding a little straight pork fat or pork belly to aid flavor and moisture.

There are plenty of options for adding even more flavor to the meatballs. **Fresh and dried herbs give flavor and color, as do chiles, spices, mustards, and mayos.**

I always use eggs in the mixture. I find they not only help bind the ingredients together, but also add a level of fat and richness, giving a velvety texture.

The size of the meatballs is the next thing to think about. I mainly make the balls the same size as a golfball and that is the size I serve. I find packing a #20 Disher ice cream scoop with meat mixture is enough for a golfball-sized meatball each time, which can help speed up your balling considerably. In my recipes I give the cooking times for that size unless otherwise stated, but feel free to pick whatever size you want. The smaller the balls, the less time they need to cook, so adjust the timings accordingly if you are making bite-sized snacks.

When it comes to rolling, wet your hands to stop the mix from sticking to them, and be sure to pack each ball firmly before rolling it between your palms.

Finally, the cooking-method debate. Frying, braising, baking—each method has its merits. For the most part I bake my balls and will challenge any diehard "pan-fry only" campaigners to come down and fry a batch of 2,000 balls in a skillet. Baking provides a controlled way of evenly cooking the balls through (if your oven is any good), after which you can add them to a sauce. Frying in small batches does give the balls a delicious, caramelized exterior, and deep-frying the balls in panko crumbs gives them a golden crunch. I have in most cases given instructions for baking the balls, but feel free to change and experiment.

Resting the mixture for 30 minutes before cooking helps the ingredients and flavors mingle. Once a mixture is made it is fine to keep it in the fridge for 24 hours before cooking.

Once cooked, the balls can be refrigerated for up to 3 days and eaten cold or reheated either in a sauce, gently simmering for 15 minutes, or in a pan with ¼ cup of light stock. Alternatively, you can reheat them for 20 minutes in the oven at 350°F, or in a microwave (following user instructions). Balls can also be frozen for up to 2 months, but make sure you defrost them fully before reheating them, being extra careful with poultry.

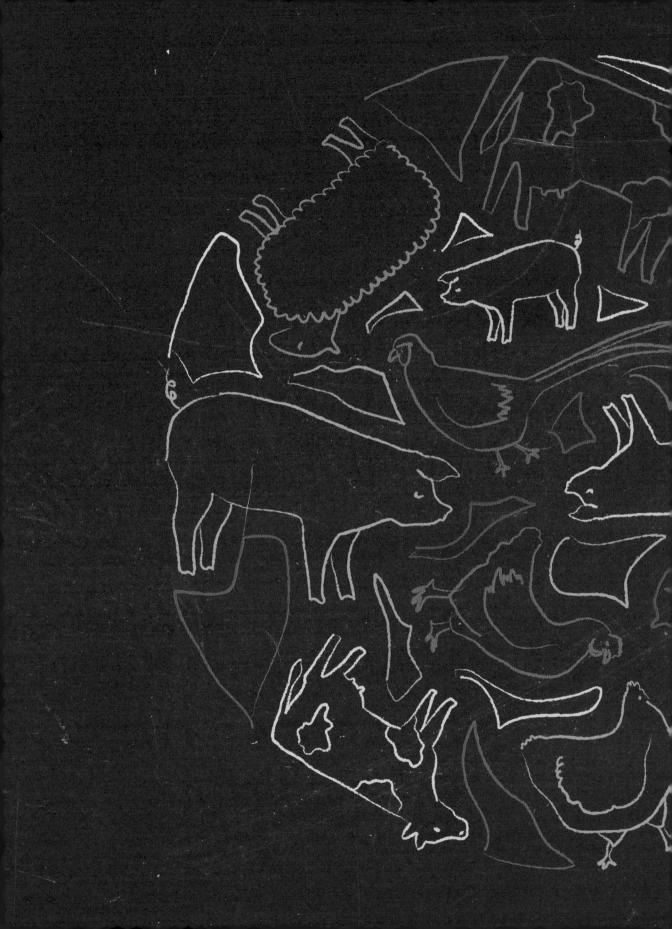

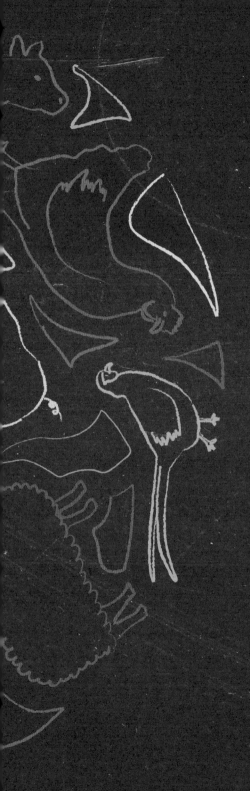

1. Meatballs

Serves
4–6

Pork & Fennel Meatballs

Pork and fennel is a classic Italian combination, and in meatballing circles they're in regular contact. This is a recipe where I've decided to soak bread in milk, instead of using a dry crumb. It helps give lightness to quite a dense mix.

2 slices (about 3½oz) stale white bread, crusts removed

scant ½ cup milk

3 teaspoons fennel seeds

1 free-range egg

3½ oz pancetta, diced

1lb boneless pork shoulder, ground

1 onion, minced

2 tablespoons chopped flat-leaf parsley

1 teaspoon salt

Preheat the oven to 425°F and line a large baking pan with nonstick parchment paper.

Roughly tear up the bread and place it in a bowl. Pour in the milk and set the bowl aside for 10–15 minutes.

Heat a heavy nonstick skillet over medium heat until it begins to smoke, then add the fennel seeds. Toast them for around 30 seconds, or until they begin to brown and start to give off a fragrant aroma. Grind them finely in a mortar and pestle.

Beat the egg in a large mixing bowl. Mash the bread and milk mixture to a paste with a fork, then combine with the egg. Add all the other ingredients and mix with your hands until well combined. This is a pretty dense mixture, so give it a good squeeze through your fingers to make sure everything gets distributed evenly.

Heat a small skillet over high heat. Break off a small amount of the mixture, flatten between your fingers, and fry until cooked. Taste to check the seasoning and add more salt if necessary. Form the mixture into 16–18 balls, each 2 inches in diameter, packing each one firmly, and place them on the prepared baking pan.

Bake for 15–18 minutes, turning the pan around halfway through—the balls should begin to brown on the top. Keep an eye on them to make sure they don't burn underneath.

Great served in a small crusty baguette, with Simple Tomato Sauce (see page 99) and some mozzarella cheese melted on top.

A variation on this recipe is to go "Pork 'n' Puy"—brown the balls in a skillet, rather than in the oven, then drop them into simmering Puy lentils for 10 minutes to finish cooking (see steps 1–2 on page 135 for how to cook lentils). You may need to add a little more vegetable or chicken stock or water. Garnish with shavings of Parmesan instead of mozzarella, and serve with crusty bread and butter.

Serves
4–6

Vietnamese Noodle Soup with Pork Balls

THE BALLS

1 large free-range egg

2 tablespoons all-purpose flour

1lb boneless pork shoulder, ground

2 scallions, thinly sliced

1 tablespoon chopped cilantro

2 tablespoons grated fresh ginger

3 tablespoons Nuoc Cham
(see page 119)

2 tablespoons olive oil

4 pints Chicken Stock (see page 90)

1 stick of cinnamon

4 scallions, sliced lengthwise

1 x 2in piece of fresh ginger, peeled
and thinly sliced

2 teaspoons sugar

1 teaspoon salt

2 tablespoons fish sauce

1 star anise

7–10oz rice vermicelli noodles
(allow 2oz dried weight per person)

1 red Thai chile, seeded and sliced

2 tablespoons soy sauce

3 shallots, thinly sliced

1½ cups beansprouts, blanched

Whenever I travel abroad now, I always try to factor in a visit to a local cooking class. It's a great way to get an insight into the food culture of a country, find out about new ingredients, and come away with a few handy tips. I went to Vietnam on my honeymoon and couldn't move for pork balls, especially in soups, skewers, and grilled. Here I have added some into a fairly traditional Vietnamese noodle soup that would be eaten day, night, and even for breakfast.

Beat the egg with the all-purpose flour in a large mixing bowl. Add the ground pork, scallions, cilantro, ginger, and Nuoc Cham and mix with your hands until well combined.

Heat a small skillet over high heat. Break off a small amount of the mixture, flatten between your fingers, and fry until cooked. Taste to check the seasoning and add more if necessary. Form the mixture into 16–18 balls, each 1½ inches in diameter, packing each one firmly.

Heat the oil in a heavy skillet and add the balls in batches so as not to overcrowd the skillet. Brown the balls for 3 minutes on each side, then remove them from the skillet and set aside.

In a large pan, add the Chicken Stock, cinnamon, scallions, fresh ginger, sugar, salt, fish sauce, and star anise, then bring to a boil. Reduce the heat and simmer for 40 minutes to let the flavors infuse. Strain the broth into another pan and taste for flavor—you can add a little Nuoc Cham if it needs a boost. Turn the heat back on, drop in the pork balls, and simmer for 15 minutes, or until the balls are cooked through.

Meanwhile, drop the noodles into a pan of boiling water and cook for 2 minutes, then drain, refresh under cold water, and drain again. Pour the soy sauce into a little dish and add the sliced chile.

Drop the beansprouts into a saucepan of boiling water. Return to boiling. Cook for 1 minute, then drain, refresh in ice cold water, and drain again.

Divide the noodles, shallots, and beansprouts between your serving bowls, then pour in the broth and balls and garnish with cilantro, basil, and a wedge of lime. Serve the chile soy sauce on the side to mix in if you require an extra flavor kick.

Serves
4–6

Mexballs

The slow-cooked Mexican dish, pork carnitas, is my favorite taco filling. Here, I have taken
a few of their ingredients and flavors and put them in the round. These Mexballs are great in
a meatball burrito.

3 tablespoons olive oil

½ a small onion, minced

1 fennel bulb, finely diced

1 garlic clove, crushed

1 teaspoon ground cumin

1 teaspoon smoked paprika

½ teaspoon ground cinnamon

1 free-range egg

3 tablespoons heavy cream

1lb boneless pork shoulder, ground

2 tablespoons fresh lime juice

1 teaspoon dried red pepper flakes

½ teaspoon chipotle paste

½ teaspoon dried oregano

3 tablespoons finely chopped
cilantro, including stalks

1 teaspoon salt

1½ cups breadcrumbs

Preheat the oven to 425°F and line a large baking pan with nonstick
parchment paper.

Heat the oil in a large heavy skillet. Add the onion and fennel and cook over low
heat for 5 minutes. Add the garlic, cumin, smoked paprika, and cinnamon.
Cook for a further 2 minutes, or until the onion is soft and translucent.

Break the egg into a large bowl. Add the cream and whisk lightly with a fork.
Add the ground pork, lime juice, dried red pepper flakes, chipotle paste,
oregano, cilantro, salt, and breadcrumbs, then add the onion and fennel
mixture and mix with your hands until well combined.

Heat a small skillet over high heat. Break off a small amount of the
mixture, flatten between your fingers, and fry until cooked. Taste to check
the seasoning and spice levels and add more if necessary. Form the mixture
into about 18 meatballs, each 2 inches in diameter, packing each one firmly,
and place them on the prepared baking pan.

Bake for 18–20 minutes, turning the pan around halfway through—the
balls should begin to brown on the top. Keep an eye on them to make sure
they don't burn underneath.

Serve in the Luardos Meatball Burrito (see page 22), or just on their own
with Tomato Salsa and Cumin Sour Cream to dip (see pages 107 and 111),
and tortilla chips to crunch on.

Serves
6

Luardos Meatball Burrito

I first met Simon Luard of Luardos at a pop-up chili-cooking competition hosted by @tweat_up. It was in the Tramshed in Shoreditch, in London, where Mark Hix now has his restaurant. We were both parked indoors; The Lawn Ranger was opposite Simon's pink, graffiti-covered van, Mary, who was luring the overfed to try a fish taco. Luardos also serve Mexican burritos out of Mary, and from Jesus, which is parked at the Whitecross Street Market. (Whitecross Street has a great selection of top food traders, if you are ever in London and want to treat your taste buds.) It wasn't long before we started experimenting with a few meatball burrito combos, and Simon has let me in on all the elements that make up the perfect burrito. Enjoy. A warning: start your beans the day before.

8oz black turtle beans, soaked overnight

1lb long-grain rice

¾ cup loosely packed grated Monterey Jack cheese or medium Cheddar

12 Mexballs (see page 21), cooked and warmed through

6 tablespoons chopped cilantro

1¾ cups Chipotle Tomato Sauce (see page 98)

½ cup Tomato Salsa (see page 107)

¾ cup Guacamole (see page 104)

½ a white cabbage, finely shredded

½ cup sour cream

6 large flour tortillas

sea salt

Soak the beans overnight. Drain them, then place them in a large pan of fresh water. Bring to a boil, then cook until the beans are soft, about an hour, once the water is boiling. Season with sea salt after they are cooked, not before or during, otherwise the beans won't soften.

Meanwhile, cook the rice according to the package instructions.

Now get all the ingredients in a line so that they are easy to add to the tortillas in the right order. For us it goes: cheese, rice, black beans, meatballs, chopped cilantro, chipotle tomato sauce, tomato salsa, guacamole, shredded cabbage, and sour cream.

Toast a tortilla in a large dry skillet until slightly brown but not crisp (it still needs to be pliable for wrapping). Add the grated cheese while it's toasting, to get the cheese melting.

One by one, add the burrito ingredients—we've suggested some amounts, but really, just add as much or as little as you prefer. Once it's all done, either wrap it up in foil or place it just as it is on a plate and eat it before it all falls apart—it's probably going to get messy. Make the rest of the burritos the same way.

Best served with a cold beer and a roll of paper towels.

Serves
6

Balls on the Line

This is the best way to prepare meatballs for the barbecue, and can be used for all the different types. Make sure you soak the wooden skewers in water before you use them, otherwise they will catch fire.

2 tablespoons olive oil

3 shallots, finely diced

2 garlic cloves, crushed

scant ½ cup ricotta cheese

1 large free-range egg

2 tablespoons heavy cream

1lb boneless beef chuck, ground

1 cup breadcrumbs

2 tablespoons wholegrain mustard

2 teaspoons chopped thyme

¼ teaspoon dried red pepper flakes

salt and freshly ground black pepper

Fire up the barbecue. Alternatively, after making the balls, turn the broiler on, or preheat the oven to 425°F, and line a baking pan with nonstick parchment paper. Place 6 wooden skewers in water to soak.

Heat the oil in a heavy skillet and add the shallots and a good pinch of salt and pepper. Cook over low heat for 3 minutes, then add the garlic and cook for another 3 minutes, or until the shallots are soft and translucent.

Put the ricotta, egg, and cream into a large bowl and mix together, breaking up the lumps of ricotta.

Add the shallots and garlic to the ricotta mixture along with the ground beef, breadcrumbs, mustard, thyme, dried red pepper flakes, and 1 teaspoon of salt. Mix with your hands until well combined.

Heat a small skillet over high heat. Break off a small amount of the mixture, flatten between your fingers and fry until cooked. Taste to check the seasoning and add more salt and red pepper flakes if necessary. Form the mixture into 18 meatballs, each about 2 inches in diameter, packing each one firmly. Then thread 3 onto each soaked skewer.

Leave to chill and firm up in the fridge for 30 minutes, then brush with a little olive oil and grill on the barbecue. Turn the skewers as you go so the balls cook through evenly and brown up on the outside. Alternatively, you can cook them under the broiler, or put them on the prepared baking pan and bake in the oven for 15–20 minutes, turning the pan around halfway through and keeping an eye on them to make sure they don't burn underneath.

Delicious with mustard or horseradish mayonnaise and a crunchy salad.

Serves
6

Ball Shiitake

Beef and mushrooms are a classic combination. The meatiness of the shiitake mushrooms
used in this recipe works really well in a meatball. Fry the mushrooms well to cook out their
high water content. If you are cooking a lot of mushrooms together it's best to work in batches
to avoid overcrowding your skillet and waterlogging the mushrooms.

1 tablespoon butter

1 large onion, minced

1 tablespoon liquid honey

1 teaspoon apple cider vinegar

10oz shiitake mushrooms, diced

1 garlic clove, crushed

2 large free-range eggs

2¼lb boneless beef chuck, finely
ground

heaped ½ cup ricotta cheese

1 tablespoon finely chopped thyme

1 tablespoon finely chopped
flat-leaf parsley

1¼ cups breadcrumbs

¼ cup milk

sea salt and freshly ground
black pepper

Preheat the oven to 425°F and line 2 large baking pans with nonstick
parchment paper.

Put a heavy skillet on medium heat and add the butter. Heat until it starts
to foam, then add the onions and a good pinch of salt and pepper. Cook on
low heat for 5 minutes, then add the honey and vinegar and cook slowly for
a further 10 minutes, or until the onion is soft, sticky, and translucent.

Add the mushrooms and garlic to the skillet, stir, and cook for 7–10 minutes,
or until the mushrooms begin to brown and any liquid has evaporated.
Remove the pan from the heat and set aside to cool.

Beat the eggs in a large mixing bowl, then add the ground beef, the cooled
mushroom and onion mix, the ricotta, thyme, parsley, breadcrumbs, milk,
and 2 teaspoons of salt. Mix everything together with your hands.

Heat a small skillet over high heat. Break off a small amount of the mixture,
flatten between your fingers, and fry until cooked. Taste to check the
seasoning and add more salt if necessary. Form the mixture into 18 balls,
each about 1½–2 inches in diameter, packing each one firmly, and place
them on the prepared baking pans.

Bake in the oven for 15–20 minutes, turning the pans around halfway
through—the balls should begin to brown on top. Keep an eye on them
to make sure that they don't burn underneath.

Serve with Asian Greens (see page 152), and rice or noodles.

Serves
6–8

Beef & Chorizo Balls

Chorizo is one of my favorite ingredients. I love it. Sweet, spicy, and smoky.
I always keep a cooking chorizo on hand to add to just about anything, in order to take it to
the next level. You can finely slice or dice chorizo, or fry it until crisp and use it like a crouton
on soups or in salads, or add it to a sandwich. It makes a great partner to beef, so it was
thrown into the mixer for this recipe early on.

2 tablespoons olive oil

2 shallots, minced

1 garlic clove, crushed

1 large free-range egg

1lb boneless beef chuck, ground

7oz cooking chorizo, sweet or spicy, finely diced

2¼ cups cooked white rice

7oz Manchego cheese, coarsely grated

1 teaspoon smoked paprika

1 cup breadcrumbs

grated zest of 1 lemon

1 teaspoon salt

3 tablespoons chopped parsley

Preheat the oven to 425°F and line 2 baking pans with nonstick parchment paper.

Heat the oil in a large heavy skillet. Add the shallots and cook on low heat for 2 minutes. Add the garlic and cook for another 5 minutes, or until the shallots are soft and translucent.

Beat the egg in a large bowl. Add the ground beef, shallots, garlic, chorizo, rice, cheese, smoked paprika, breadcrumbs, lemon zest, salt, and parsley. Mix with your hands until well combined.

Heat a small skillet over high heat. Break off a small amount of the mixture, flatten between your fingers, and fry until cooked. Taste to check the seasoning and add more if necessary. Form the mixture into 28–30 balls, each about 2 inches in diameter, packing each one firmly, and place them on the prepared baking pans.

Bake for 18–20 minutes, turning the pans around halfway through—the balls should begin to brown on the top. Keep an eye on them to make sure they don't burn underneath.

I often serve these Bun 'n' Ball style. Get a bun or roll of your choosing (I like a toasted ciabatta or brioche burger bun). Then spread on some Confit Garlic Mayonnaise (see page 115), add some green leaves (arugula, etc.), sliced gherkins, or Pickled Cucumber (see page 148), and some cheese you can melt under a broiler or serve grated on top. Devour, but be sure to have some napkins on hand.

Serves
4–6

Sweaty Balls

Quite simply, these balls are going to make you sweat.
A stalwart of the London street food scene, "The Rib Man," aka Mark Gevaux, has been selling
his barbecue baby back ribs around London's Brick Lane area with huge success.
I love his mind-blowing hot sauces made from a combination of Scotch Bonnet and
Naga Jolokia chile peppers. Here, you can use any ready-made hot sauce of your choice to
give the balls a boom, with the Cheddar flavor following once the heat subsides.

1–2 tablespoons olive oil

½ an onion, minced

1 garlic clove, crushed

2 tablespoons tomato paste

2 free-range eggs

**4oz Cheddar cheese,
coarsely grated**

1lb boneless beef chuck, ground

1 cup breadcrumbs

1 teaspoon salt

**3 tablespoons finely chopped
oregano**

**3 tablespoons finely chopped
flat-leaf parsley**

**3 tablespoons ready-made hot sauce
of your choice**

Preheat the oven to 425°F and line a large baking pan with nonstick parchment paper.

Heat the oil in a large heavy skillet. Add the onion and cook on low heat for 2 minutes. Add the garlic and cook on low heat for 3 more minutes, or until the onion is translucent. Then add the tomato paste and keep cooking and stirring for 2 minutes.

Remove from the heat and allow to cool a little. Beat the eggs in a large mixing bowl and add all the rest of the ingredients, including the cooled onion mixture. Mix with your hands until well combined.

Heat a small skillet over high heat. Break off a small amount of the mixture, flatten between your fingers, and fry until cooked. Taste to check the seasoning and spiciness, and add more if necessary. Form the mixture into about 18 meatballs, each 2 inches in diameter, packing each one firmly, and place them on the prepared pan.

Bake for 15–18 minutes, turning the pan around halfway through—the balls should begin to brown on the top. Keep an eye on them to make sure they don't burn underneath.

I suggest having some Cumin Sour Cream (see page 111) or Greek-style yogurt on standby to put the flames out, and wearing a sweatband on your head to catch that perspiration.

Serves
4–6

Sticky Balls

These balls are sticky because of the sweet honey and garlic sauce they are served with, which makes them perfect for little ballers. Try getting the kids to wrap these balls inside an iceberg lettuce leaf, to get some crunchy fresh vegetables into them.

3 tablespoons olive oil

1 onion, minced

1 tablespoon tomato paste

2 free-range eggs

½lb boneless pork shoulder, ground

½lb boneless beef chuck, ground

4 garlic cloves, crushed

1 tablespoon Dijon mustard

1 tablespoon Worcestershire sauce

1½ cups breadcrumbs

2 teaspoons sea salt

1 x recipe Honey & Garlic Sticky Ball Sauce (see page 96)

chopped chives, to garnish

Preheat the oven to 425°F and line a large baking pan with nonstick parchment paper.

To make the balls, heat the oil in a heavy skillet over medium heat. Add the onions, turn the heat to low, and cook for 5 minutes until they turn translucent. Add the tomato paste and cook for a further 2 minutes. Set aside to cool.

Beat the eggs in a large bowl, then add the ground pork and beef, garlic, mustard, Worcestershire sauce, breadcrumbs, and salt, and mix with your hands until well combined.

Heat a small skillet over high heat. Break off a small amount of the mixture, flatten between your fingers, and fry until cooked. Taste to check the seasoning and add more if necessary. Form the mixture into about 20 balls, each 2 inches in diameter, packing each one firmly, and place them on the prepared baking pan.

Bake for 15–18 minutes, turning the pan around halfway through—the balls should begin to brown on the top. Keep an eye on them to make sure they don't burn underneath.

Heat the sauce through gently in a large saucepan. Add the balls and simmer for 2 minutes. Scatter with the chopped chives and serve.

Some Pickled Carrot & Daikon (see page 148) is nice on the side, to cut through the sweetness.

Serves
4–6

Great Balls of Fire

This is the first ball I developed and the first ball I served to a member of the paying public. It was the moment when things really started to roll, with my cooking truly exposed and the adrenaline pumping. It felt good. This is a ball with plenty of flavor and texture, and I like to load up the red pepper flakes to increase the fire. They can take a good braise in any sauce but I serve them in my spiced tomato and red onion sauce.

scant ½ cup ricotta cheese

2 free-range eggs

13oz boneless pork shoulder, finely ground

7oz boneless beef chuck, finely ground

1¾ cups Japanese panko breadcrumbs (or 1¼ cups fresh breadcrumbs)

2 garlic cloves, crushed

3 tablespoons finely chopped cilantro stems, leaves reserved

2 teaspoons sea salt

½ teaspoon dried red pepper flakes

1 x recipe Spiced Red Onion & Tomato Sauce (see page 100)

Preheat the oven to 425°F and line a large baking pan with nonstick parchment paper.

Put the ricotta into a large bowl and break it up using a fork. Add the eggs and whisk together. Add the ground pork and beef, panko crumbs (or fresh breadcrumbs), garlic, cilantro stems, salt, and dried red pepper flakes. Mix with your hands until well combined.

Heat a small skillet over high heat. Break off a small amount of the mixture, flatten between your fingers, and fry until cooked. Taste to check the seasoning and spice levels and add more salt and dried red pepper flakes, if necessary. Form the mixture into about 18 balls, each 1½–2 inches in diameter, packing each one firmly, and place them on the prepared baking pan.

Bake in the oven for 15–18 minutes, turning the pan around halfway through—the balls should begin to brown on the top. Keep an eye on them to make sure they don't burn underneath.

Meanwhile, heat the sauce in a large pan over medium heat. When the balls are cooked, add them to the sauce and simmer for 15 minutes.

Scatter with a few leaves of cilantro, and serve with sour cream and a baby spinach and arugula salad on the side.

Serves
4–6

The Popeye

Who likes spinach? And who's been brought up thinking that eating it gives you superhuman powers? Popeye had a lot to do with instilling that belief in me. In fact, my great-grandfather was a sailor and had tattoos just like him. So this ball goes out to the spinach lovers. I use fresh spinach here, rather than Popeye's canned stuff. I also find it easier to eat with a fork rather than sucking it through a pipe, but each to their own.

1lb fresh spinach, large stems discarded

2 tablespoons olive oil

1 large onion, minced

2 garlic cloves, crushed

1 large free-range egg

2 tablespoons milk

¾ cup fresh breadcrumbs

2oz Parmesan cheese, finely grated

2 tablespoons finely chopped flat-leaf parsley

2 tablespoons finely chopped fresh oregano, or 1 teaspoon dried oregano

10oz boneless pork shoulder, ground

10oz boneless beef chuck, ground

sea salt and freshly ground black pepper

Preheat the oven to 425°F and line a large baking pan with nonstick parchment paper.

Wash the spinach, then place it in a large pan and add a splash of water. Cook over high heat, stirring, until the spinach has wilted and softened. Squeeze it between two plates to get rid of any excess liquid, then chop it finely.

Put the olive oil into a heavy skillet over medium heat. Add the onion, garlic, black pepper, and 2 teaspoons of salt. Stir over low heat for 6 minutes, or until the onion becomes translucent, being careful not to burn the garlic (add a splash more oil if things look like they are sticking). Add the spinach and cook, stirring, for a further 2 minutes. Then remove from the heat and leave to cool to room temperature.

Beat together the egg and milk in a large mixing bowl, then add the breadcrumbs, Parmesan, parsley, oregano, and a pinch of salt. Stir to combine. Add the ground pork and beef and the spinach and onion mixture. Mix with your hands until well combined.

Heat a small skillet over high heat. Break off a small amount of the mixture, flatten between your fingers, and fry until cooked. Taste to check the seasoning and add more salt and pepper if necessary. Form the mixture into about 20 meatballs, each 2 inches in diameter, packing each one firmly, and place them on the prepared baking pan.

Bake for 15–20 minutes, turning the pan around halfway through—the balls should begin to brown on the top. Keep an eye on them to make sure they don't burn underneath.

Serve the balls with Simple Tomato Sauce on the side for dipping (see page 99), or with potatoes mashed with mustard, and a green salad.

Makes
6–7

Homeslice Meatball Calzone

In their own words, "Homeslice is the love child of three men with a passion for making and eating wood-fired pizza." I met this Kiwi threesome early on in Bowler life. Hugging their homemade wood-fired oven-cum-trailer is a great way to keep warm on a cold evening. Their pizzas are stunning—light with a crisp base—and I'm thrilled they've shared a little doughy delight here.

1 cup warm water

2 tablespoons soft brown sugar

2 teaspoons baker's active dried yeast

5 cups bread flour

1 heaped tablespoon sea salt (Maldon recommended)

½ cup butter, melted

6–7 cooked Bowler meatballs and sauce of your choice

freshly grated mozzarella cheese

sliced scallions

Put the water into a bowl and add the sugar. Stir until dissolved, then add the yeast and cover the bowl. Leave in a warm place for 5 minutes, until the mixture is foamy.

Put the flour and salt into a mixing bowl and stir in the melted butter and the yeast mixture. Once it comes together as dough, turn it out onto a floured work surface. Knead well for 10–15 minutes (don't slack!), adding more flour as needed. The dough shouldn't stick to your hands but should cling to itself—the more you mix it the wetter it will feel. Once kneaded, place the dough back in the bowl and cover with a cloth. Let it sit in a warm place for 40 minutes or so, until it has almost doubled in size.

Divide the risen dough into 6 or 7 portions and roll each into a tight ball. Place the balls on a baking pan, cover with plastic wrap, and leave in a cool place for an hour. It will now be ready to roll out, but your window for use is getting small. If you are making your dough earlier in the day you can keep the balls in the fridge, but bring them out about 20–30 minutes before use.

Heat the oven to 425°F. Flour your board and, if you're a hands-on person, you can stretch and roll the dough into a circle using your hands; however, using a rolling pin is a viable option. Roll the dough as thinly as you can without splitting it, making circles 6–8 inches across and ¼ inch deep.

Place a meatball on one half of your dough circle, adding the sauce of your choice. I recommend a Beef & Chorizo Ball (see page 28) with Chipotle Tomato Sauce (see page 98). Scatter with some grated mozzarella and sliced scallions. To seal the calzone, take a brush or your finger and spread sauce thinly around the edge of the dough circle. Fold the empty half of the circle over the filling, press together, and pinch the edges firmly together. The better the seal here the more it will puff and look delicious.

Place the calzones on a baking pan. Bake for 5–10 minutes, or until starting to color. Don't leave them too long or you'll end up with dry calzone. Serve straight from the oven. They're best served as an appetizer.

Serves
5–6

Smokin' Bacon Balls

There were four hours to go before I was expected at a private party Richard Bacon was throwing in his back garden, for which I'd been asked to do the food. Exciting stuff. I had some chuck steak in the fridge along with some smoked lardons. "Rude not to," I thought, turning the oven on.

1 tablespoon olive oil

7oz oak-smoked bacon lardons

1½ cups breadcrumbs

2 free-range eggs

scant ½ cup heavy cream

7oz ricotta cheese

1½lb boneless beef chuck, ground

5oz smoked Cheddar, shredded

1 teaspoon smoked paprika

2 teaspoons salt

2 tablespoons chopped
flat-leaf parsley

Preheat the oven to 425°F and line 2 large baking pans with nonstick parchment paper. If you only have a single baking pan, you will need to cook the balls in batches.

Heat the oil in a large heavy skillet. Add the bacon lardons and cook on medium heat for 5 minutes, or until they are crisp.

Put the breadcrumbs into a mixing bowl. Using a slotted spoon, transfer the lardons from the skillet to a cutting board and pour the juices and oil from the skillet into the breadcrumbs. Chop the lardons finely, then add them to the breadcrumb mixture and allow to cool.

Beat the eggs and cream in a large mixing bowl, then add the ricotta, stirring well to break up any large lumps. Add all the rest of the ingredients and mix with your hands until well combined.

Heat a small skillet over high heat. Break off a small amount of the mixture, flatten between your fingers, and fry until cooked. Taste to check the seasoning and the smokiness and add more salt, pepper, and paprika if necessary. Form the mixture into 30 balls, each 2 inches in diameter, packing each one firmly. Place them on the prepared baking pans.

Bake for 15–18 minutes, turning the pans around halfway through—the balls should begin to brown on the top. Keep an eye on them to make sure they don't burn underneath.

A delicious way to gain weight, served with a Simple Tomato Sauce (see page 99) and a slab of Potato Rösti (see page 131), or try them with a fried egg and some Wild Mushroom Sauce (see page 92) or hollandaise.

Hawksmoor's Meatballs & Grits

Hawksmoor, in my opinion, is the best steak restaurant in London.
It's all about the meat, with complete commitment to finding the best British cuts available. This is also at the heart of great meatballing. I've followed Hawksmoor owners Huw and Will's rise to the top of the meaty food chain, I've listened to their advice, as well as their sublime karaoke singing, and I'm thrilled that they have let me have their own meatball recipe.

1 large free-range egg, beaten

1lb ground pork

1lb ground beef

1 garlic clove, chopped

¼ cup white wine

2oz Stilton cheese, grated

½ cup all-purpose flour, for dusting

olive oil, for frying

**sea salt and freshly ground
black pepper**

TO GARNISH

10 sage leaves

a handful of large capers

Preheat the oven to 300°F.

To make the meatballs, beat the egg in a large bowl. Mix in the ground meat, garlic, egg, wine, Stilton cheese, salt, and pepper. Form the mixture into 25 balls, each 2 inches in diameter, and dust each one with some flour.

Fry the balls in oil for about 15 minutes, or until golden. Do this in several batches because if you overcrowd the skillet it will be hard to get them to brown evenly, and they may break up when you are turning them. Once cooked, place the balls in a Dutch oven.

THE SAUCE

1 small onion, minced

5 large, fat garlic cloves, crushed

½ a red chile, roughly chopped

1 carrot, chopped

2 tablespoons olive oil

2 cups chicken gravy (chicken stock reduced by half)

2 cups beef gravy (beef stock reduced by half)

1lb can diced tomatoes

In the same skillet, fry the onion, garlic, chile, and carrot in the olive oil. Add the mixture to the Dutch oven with the meatballs. Pour in the chicken and beef gravies and the diced tomatoes, then season to taste with salt and pepper. Place over medium heat and bring to a simmer, then place in the oven for 1 hour. Taste and correct the seasoning if necessary.

Remove the meatballs from the Dutch oven and keep warm. Pass the sauce through a chinois or blend with an immersion hand blender, then combine the sauce and meatballs and set aside in a warm place until ready to serve.

Just before serving, fry the sage leaves and capers in a little olive oil over high heat until crisp.

To serve, place a spoonful of cheese grits or polenta into a bowl and top with the hot meatballs and a little sauce. Garnish with the fried sage leaves and capers (turn the page to see the finished result).

CHEESE GRITS

2 pints milk

1¾ cups white grits or white polenta

½ cup butter

3½oz American or Swiss cheese, shredded

3½oz Gruyère cheese, shredded

To make the cheese grits, heat the milk to a simmer in a large pan. Pour the grits or polenta into the milk in a steady stream, whisking as you go. Reduce the heat and stir steadily for 20 minutes, then stir in the butter followed by the two cheeses. Keep stirring until smooth.

Set aside and keep warm until needed.

Serves
4–6

Björn Balls

My great friend Chris fell in love with a Swedish girl, Annika. The downsides were he moved to Sweden, almost became teetotal because of the price of booze, and can now talk about us behind our backs in Swedish. The upsides are that I regularly go to one of the meatball capitals of the world, get forced to drink tasty schnapps, and have a free place to stay. There is a lot of discussion about what makes a traditional Swedish "köttbullar." This recipe contains a mix of some of my findings but I am not going to claim it's 100% traditional. It tastes great though.

2 tablespoons olive oil

1 small onion, minced

1 large free-range egg

10oz ground beef

5oz ground pork

5oz ground veal

1 cup dried breadcrumbs

¼ cup milk

1 tablespoon juice from canned Abba anchovies (optional)

¼ teaspoon ground allspice

¼ teaspoon ground nutmeg

a pinch of ground ginger

½ teaspoon freshly ground black pepper

1½ teaspoons salt

Preheat the oven to 425°F, and line a large baking pan with nonstick parchment paper.

Heat the oil in a large heavy skillet. Add the onion and cook on low heat for 5 minutes, or until the onion is soft and translucent. At this stage, I would always add a few pinches of salt and grinds of pepper so the onions are seasoned from the start, meaning that you don't have to add so much later.

Beat the egg in a large bowl. Add the ground beef, pork, and veal, the breadcrumbs, milk, anchovy juice (if using), allspice, ground nutmeg, ginger, pepper, and salt. Mix with your hands until well combined.

Heat a small skillet over high heat. Break off a small amount of the mixture, flatten between your fingers, and fry until cooked. Taste to check the seasoning and add more if necessary. Form the mixture into about 18 balls, each 2 inches in diameter, packing each one firmly, and place them on the prepared baking pan.

Bake for 18–20 minutes, turning the pan around halfway through—the balls should begin to brown on the top. Keep an eye on them to make sure they don't burn underneath. Let them rest for 2 minutes and they are good to go. Alternatively, brown the balls in olive oil in a skillet over high heat for 8–10 minutes, then drop them into a pan of simmering Crispy Cream sauce (see page 102) to finish cooking.

Traditionally, Swedish meatballs are served with boiled or mashed potatoes, lingonberry jam (if you can't get hold of lingonberry, use cranberry), cream sauce, sliced pickled cucumbers, and fresh dill, but they taste great with almost anything.

Serves
4–6

Côte de Veau Pojarski

While researching different balling ideas, I came across a classic French dish called Côte de Veau Pojarski where the meat is removed from veal chops, ground, balled, and reformed around the bone. Russian in its origin, the story goes that Pojarski, a 19th-century Russian innkeeper, made his name making tasty beef meatballs loved by Czar Nicholas. One day the Czar dropped by but there was no beef, so the dish was improvised using veal, which the Czar loved even more. Serve these to the Czars in your life.

4–6 veal chop bones (depending on how many you are serving)

3½ tablespoons butter

3 shallots, minced

1 garlic clove, crushed

1 large free-range egg

¼ pint heavy cream

1lb Prime or Choice grade boneless veal, ground

1 cup breadcrumbs

3 tablespoons finely chopped chives

1 tablespoon chopped flat-leaf parsley

1 teaspoon chopped thyme

¼ teaspoon freshly grated nutmeg

1 teaspoon salt

¼ teaspoon black pepper

finely grated zest of 1 lemon

Put the veal chop bones into a pan of boiling water for 10 minutes, then scrape everything off them so they are clean. Set them aside to dry.

Preheat the oven to 425°F.

Heat 1 heaping tablespoon of the butter in a large heavy-based pan. Add the shallots and cook on low heat for 2 minutes. Add the garlic and cook for a further 5 minutes, or until the shallots are soft and translucent. Set aside to cool slightly.

Break the egg into a large bowl, add the cream, and whisk lightly with a fork. Add the cooked shallots and garlic, ground veal, breadcrumbs, chives, parsley, thyme, nutmeg, lemon zest, salt, and pepper. Mix with your hands until well combined.

Heat a small skillet over high heat. Break off a small amount of the mixture, flatten between your fingers, and fry until cooked. Taste to check the seasoning and add more if necessary. Form the mixture into 4–6 big balls, then make a hole in each with a knife and insert a veal bone, pushing and firming the mixture around the bone.

Melt the remaining butter and pour it into an ovenproof dish. Transfer the balls to the dish and bake for 30 minutes, basting with the butter and turning the dish around halfway through—the balls should begin to brown on the top. Keep an eye on them to make sure they don't burn underneath.

When the balls are cooked, transfer them carefully from the dish onto serving plates. Support them underneath to make sure they don't split.

Mushrooms are a traditional accompaniment, so serve these balls with Wild Mushroom Sauce (see page 92), mashed celeriac, or some buttered pasta, with lemon wedges on the side.

Serves
4–6

Veal & Parmesan Balls

The consumption of veal has long been on the animal welfare agenda. However, I feel
strongly that we should eat veal, otherwise male calves—the by-product of the milk industry,
unable to give milk and not from herds bred for meat—are being killed and destroyed for
no reason. It seems like an injustice not to put the meat to good use.
When buying veal look for USDA Prime or Choice grade cuts.

3½ tablespoons butter

3 shallots, minced

1 garlic clove, crushed

2 free-range eggs

¾lb boneless Prime or Choice
grade veal, ground

¼lb boneless pork shoulder, ground

2oz Parmesan cheese, grated

1 tablespoon chopped
flat-leaf parsley

1 tablespoons finely chopped
oregano

1 teaspoon salt

¼ teaspoon black pepper

finely grated zest of 1 lime

1½ cups breadcrumbs

scant ½ cup milk

Preheat the oven to 425°F, and line a large baking pan with nonstick
parchment paper.

Heat 1 heaping tablespoon of the butter in a large heavy skillet. Add the
shallots and cook on low heat for 2 minutes. Add the garlic and cook for a
further 5 minutes, or until the shallots are soft and translucent. Toward the
end of the cooking time add the remaining butter and let it melt, then set
the skillet aside to cool slightly.

Beat the eggs in a large bowl. Add the ground veal and pork, Parmesan,
parsley, oregano, salt, pepper, and lime zest. Stir the breadcrumbs and
milk into the onions and butter, then add to the meat mixture. Mix with
your hands until well combined.

Heat a small skillet over high heat. Break off a small amount of the
mixture, flatten between your fingers, and fry until cooked. Taste to
check the seasoning and add more if necessary. Form the mixture into
18–20 balls, each 2 inches in diameter, packing each one firmly, and
place them on the prepared baking pan.

Bake for 18–20 minutes, turning the pan around halfway through—the
balls should begin to brown on the top. Keep an eye on them to make sure
they don't burn underneath.

If you need comforting, serve the balls with Wild Mushroom Sauce (see
page 92), Polenta (see page 126) and green beans, or lighten them up for
summer with a zucchini and pine nut salad.

Serves
4–6

Green Chile Chicken Balls

I love these balls because you can really taste the green chile in them—it adds a great freshness. I use chicken thighs here because they have much more flavor and the result is a lot more moist than when you use breast meat, which can sometimes dry out too quickly.

2 tablespoons olive oil

1 onion, minced

2 garlic cloves, crushed

8 fresh green chiles, seeded and minced

1 x 1¾-inch piece of fresh ginger, peeled and diced

20 cashews

3 tablespoons finely chopped cilantro, plus extra leaves to garnish

2 free-range eggs

2 tablespoons milk

1½lb boneless, skinless chicken thighs, ground

2 teaspoons Garam Masala (see page 111)

1½ cups breadcrumbs

2 teaspoons salt

freshly ground black pepper

lime wedges, to serve

Preheat the oven to 425°F, and line a large baking pan with nonstick parchment paper.

Heat the oil in a large heavy skillet. Add the onion and cook on low heat for 2 minutes. Add the garlic, chiles, ginger, and cashews, and cook on low heat for 3 more minutes, or until the onion is translucent.

Remove from the heat, allow to cool a little, then put into a food processor with the cilantro and blitz to a rough paste. You might have to add a splash of olive oil or water to help it blend properly. Beat the eggs with the milk in a large bowl, then add the paste, ground chicken, Garam Masala, breadcrumbs, salt, and pepper, and mix well.

Heat a small skillet over high heat. Break off a small amount of the mixture, flatten between your fingers, and fry until cooked. Taste to check the seasoning and add more salt and spices if necessary. Form the mixture into 20–22 meatballs, each about 2 inches in diameter, packing each one firmly, and place them on the prepared baking pan.

Bake for 15–18 minutes, turning the pan around halfway through—the balls should begin to brown on the top. Keep an eye on them to make sure they don't burn underneath.

Serve with Coconut Curry Sauce (see page 117) and steamed jasmine rice with lime wedges on the side. Garnish with Crispy Fried Shallots (see page 154) and cilantro leaves.

Serves
4–6

Steamy Chicken Balls

It's time to dust off your bamboo steamer—you know it's up on the top shelf somewhere.
This is my ball food answer to Chinese dumplings. Am convinced they're very good for you.
Anything steamed is, right?

1 large free-range egg

3 scallions, thinly sliced

2 garlic cloves, crushed

**7oz skinless, boneless chicken
breasts, ground**

**10oz skinless, boneless chicken
thighs, ground**

**1 x 1-inch piece of fresh ginger,
peeled and grated**

1 cup breadcrumbs

2 tablespoons fish sauce

1 tablespoon soy sauce

freshly ground black pepper

sesame oil, for brushing

Beat the egg in a large bowl. Add all the other ingredients, except the sesame
oil, and mix with your hands until combined. You can blitz this in a food
processor, but don't overprocess—you want to keep some texture and bite.

Heat a small skillet over high heat. Break off a small amount of the
mixture, flatten between your fingers, and fry until cooked. Taste to check
the seasoning and add more if necessary. Form the mixture into 18 small
balls, each about 1¾ inches in diameter, packing each one firmly. Chill the
balls for 15 minutes, and meanwhile bring a large pan of water to a boil.

Line the bottom of a bamboo steamer with some parchment paper, or a
banana leaf if you're feeling fancy. Then brush the balls with the sesame
oil and set them in the steamer. Place the steamer over the pan of boiling
water and steam on high heat for 15 minutes, or until the balls are
cooked through. You may have to steam the balls in two batches to avoid
overcrowding your steamer.

Serve the balls with Pickled Carrot & Daikon (page 148) and a bowl of soy
sauce with sliced red chile added, for dipping.

Serves
4

Baa Baa Balls

I was born on a British Air Force base in Cyprus, in the middle of the war in 1974.
This must have been where I developed my passion for Greek flavors, despite leaving before
I was a year old. Salty feta with full-flavored lamb and fresh mint is a classic combination and
will work just as well on a stuffed leg of lamb as it does here in a ball.

2 tablespoons olive oil

½ an onion, minced

3 garlic cloves, crushed

1 large free-range egg

3oz feta cheese, crumbled

1lb boneless lamb shoulder, ground

1 cup breadcrumbs

**2 tablespoons finely chopped
mint leaves**

1 teaspoon dried mixed herbs

1 teaspoon dried mint

½ teaspoon salt

1 tablespoon ground cumin

¼ cup heavy cream

**finely grated zest and juice
of 1 lime**

Preheat the oven to 425°F, and line a large baking pan with nonstick
parchment paper.

Heat the oil in a large heavy skillet. Add the onion and cook on low heat for
2 minutes. Add the garlic and cook for another 5 minutes, or until the onion
is soft and translucent.

Beat the egg in a large bowl. Add the feta, ground lamb, breadcrumbs, fresh
and dried herbs, salt, cumin, cream, and lime zest and juice. Mix with your
hands until well combined.

Heat a small skillet over high heat. Break off a small amount of the
mixture, flatten between your fingers, and fry until cooked. Taste to check
the seasoning and add more if necessary. Form the mixture into 16 balls,
each 2 inches in diameter, packing each one firmly, and place them on the
prepared baking pan.

Bake for 18–20 minutes, turning the pan around halfway through—the
balls should begin to brown on the top. Keep an eye on them to make sure
they don't burn underneath.

Simply serve these straight from the oven with a dipping sauce of Cumin
Sour Cream (see page 111) or Spicy Lime Yogurt (see page 113).

Serves
4–6

Ballymaloe Spicy Indian Meatballs

I had an amazing grandma. I called her GM cause she was a food-loving, white-wine drinking, Benson & Hedges-smoking, fashionable grandma. She called herself Ann because she didn't like her name, Emily. I quite like the name Emily. Still, "Grandma" seemed too old and dusty, so GM she became. When she went to the smoking room in the sky, she left me a few thousand. I could have cleared the credit card debt but that didn't feel right. I wanted to do something good, something beneficial, to learn. It was to be the greatest gift, to learn how to cook. Then a friend mentioned Ballymaloe (cheers, Mo). If you like food, want to immerse yourself in growing, cooking, and eating it for three months, then Ballymaloe is for you. Set on an organic farm near Cork, in Ireland, it is a magical place to lay some culinary foundations, fish, butcher, and forage. If you like Guinness, that's a bonus. If you like Beamish, better still. Ballymaloe. It's got a "ball" in its name and it's run by the inspirational Darina Allen, who has kindly let me have her meatball recipe.

4 green cardamom pods

1½ teaspoons coriander seeds

1 clove

14½oz ground shoulder of lamb or beef

¼–½ teaspoon chili powder

2–3 small garlic cloves, mashed

1 free-range egg

salt and freshly ground black pepper

Remove the seeds from the cardamom pods, discarding the husks. Grind the seeds in a mortar and pestle with the coriander seeds and clove, then put into a bowl with the ground meat, chili powder, egg, and mashed garlic. Mix well. Season with salt and freshly ground black pepper.

Heat a small skillet over high heat. Break off a small amount of the mixture, flatten between your fingers, and fry until cooked. Taste to check the seasoning and add more if necessary. Wet your hands with water, then form the mixture into 30–36 little meatballs, each about 1¾ inches in diameter.

Cover and chill until required, or cook immediately either on a barbecue or over medium heat in a lightly oiled skillet. They will take a couple of minutes on each side.

Provide toothpicks or thread the cooked balls onto satay sticks, and serve with Darina's Pomegranate Seed & Cilantro Raita (see page 121).

Lamb, Rosemary & Garlic Meatballs

Lamb, rosemary, and garlic is a well-loved combination and now it's in ball form. Rosemary is such a hardy herb. Often it's used as a decorative plant, and I have, on the odd occasion, been known to do a bit of neighborly "driveway foraging" for an emergency sprig.

2 tablespoons olive oil

1 large onion, finely diced

4 garlic cloves, crushed

1 large free-range egg

1lb boneless lamb shoulder, ground

1 cup breadcrumbs

2 tablespoons finely chopped rosemary

2 tablespoons finely chopped flat-leaf parsley

2 teaspoons wholegrain mustard

zest of 1 lemon

1 tablespoon freshly squeezed lemon juice

1 teaspoon salt

freshly ground black pepper

Preheat the oven to 425°F, and line a baking pan with nonstick parchment paper.

Heat the oil in a large heavy skillet. Add the onions and cook on low heat for 2 minutes. Add the garlic and continue to cook on low heat for 3 more minutes, or until the onion is translucent. Remove from the heat and set aside to cool.

Beat the egg in a large mixing bowl, then add the rest of the ingredients. Mix with your hands until well combined.

Heat a small skillet over high heat. Break off a small amount of the mixture, flatten between your fingers, and fry until cooked. Taste to check the seasoning and add more if necessary. Form the mixture into 16 balls, each about 2 inches in diameter, packing each one firmly, and place them on the prepared baking pan.

Bake for 15–18 minutes, turning the pan around halfway through—the balls should begin to brown on the top. Keep an eye on them to make sure the balls don't burn underneath.

I like to serve these Pudding Bowler style (see page 132) with Red Wine Gravy (see page 90), and Honey-roasted Vegetables (see page 151).

Serves
4–6

Lamb, Goat Cheese & Caramelized Onion Balls

We were asked to bring our balls to the Imperial Arms pub on the King's Road in Chelsea, in London, to do a pop-up residency. It was spring, so I thought we had better do a seasonal ball with lamb as the star. Lamb has such a great flavor, complementing the salty sweetness of the goat cheese and onions.

1 large free-range egg

4oz Caramelized Red Onions, chopped (see page 154)

2 garlic cloves, crushed

1lb boneless lamb shoulder, ground

3½oz goat cheese, crumbled

scant ½ cup milk

1½ cups breadcrumbs

1 tablespoon finely chopped flat-leaf parsley

3 tablespoons finely chopped basil

1 teaspoon salt

¼ teaspoon freshly ground black pepper

Preheat the oven to 425°F, and line a large baking pan with nonstick parchment paper.

Beat the egg into a large bowl. Add all of the other ingredients and mix everything together with your hands until well combined.

Heat a small skillet over high heat. Break off a small amount of the mixture, flatten between your fingers, and fry until cooked. Taste to check the seasoning and add more if necessary. Form the mixture into 18 meatballs, each about 2 inches in diameter, packing each one firmly, and place them on the prepared baking pan.

Bake for 18–20 minutes, turning the pan around halfway through—the balls should begin to brown on the top. Keep an eye on them to make sure they don't burn underneath.

Serve with Citrus Couscous (see page 147) and Honey-roasted Vegetables (see page 151). Any leftovers are just as nice cold for a super-charged packed lunch that will turn your colleagues green with envy.

Serves
6

Ball Games—Game Balls

Occasionally I am lucky enough to be given a pheasant or a partridge, and I've come up with this recipe as a result. I've been getting into butchery, and I prefer to take the breasts from the birds without plucking them first. Otherwise it's a bit messy plucking a whole bird at home without the neighbors thinking a lunatic is on the loose. Your butcher can easily do it for you.

½ cup dried pears

2 free-range eggs

1 cup dried breadcrumbs

1lb pheasant breast meat, boned and ground

8oz pork fatback, ground

¾ cup heavy cream

2 tablespoons chopped flat-leaf parsley

1 garlic clove, crushed

1 teaspoon salt

freshly ground black pepper

Soak the dried pears in warm water for 15 minutes, then drain and dice.

Preheat the oven to 425°F, and line 2 baking pans with nonstick parchment paper.

Lightly whisk the eggs in a large mixing bowl. In a separate bowl, mix together the diced pears and breadcrumbs (these will stop the chopped pears from sticking together). Add the pear and breadcrumb mixture to the eggs, then stir in the ground pheasant and fatback, cream, parsley, garlic, and salt. The mixture will initially seem very wet and will remain sticky. Just keep mixing (using your hands is easiest) and you will find that the breadcrumbs will absorb the cream.

Heat a small skillet over high heat. Break off a small amount of the mixture, flatten between your fingers, and fry until cooked. Taste to check the seasoning and add pepper and more salt if necessary.

Form the mixture into about 20–24 balls, each 2 inches in diameter, packing each one firmly, and place them on the prepared baking pans.

Bake for 15–20 minutes, turning the pans around halfway through—the balls should begin to brown on the top. Keep an eye on them to make sure they don't burn underneath.

These are nice served with Wild Mushroom Sauce (see page 92), mashed potatoes, and sautéed Savoy cabbage.

2. Fish Balls

Serves
4–6

Wasabi Salmon & Sesame Seed Balls

Wasabi is a Japanese root and comes from the same family as horseradish. When I first saw it I was surprised to find that it isn't green, as the dye in many store-bought varieties may lead you to believe. I love the hit you get from having slightly too much wasabi; when it connects with the roof of your mouth—eye watering, brain tingling, and sinus-cleansingly great. I have increased my tolerance over time, taking the pain along the way. I love it with salmon, so I had to use it in this recipe. Be careful not to overcook the salmon otherwise it will dry out.

1lb skinless salmon fillet

1 medium free-range egg

3 scallions, thinly sliced

1 tablespoon diced pickled ginger

1 teaspoon wasabi powder

2 tablespoons chopped cilantro

1 tablespoon freshly squeezed lemon juice

1 tablespoon soy sauce or tamari

1 cup breadcrumbs

1 teaspoon salt

freshly ground black pepper

3 tablespoons black sesame seeds, toasted

3 tablespoons white sesame seeds, toasted

Preheat the oven to 425°F, and line a large baking pan with nonstick parchment paper.

Cut the salmon into 1-inch cubes and place in the freezer for 20 minutes. Once chilled, pulse in a food processor. Don't overprocess—you want to retain some pieces of fish for texture.

Beat the egg in a large mixing bowl. Add the scallions, pickled ginger, wasabi powder, cilantro, lemon juice, soy sauce, breadcrumbs, salt, and a sprinkling of pepper.

Heat a small skillet over high heat. Break off a small amount of the mixture, flatten between your fingers, and fry until cooked. Taste to check the seasoning and add more lemon, ginger, or wasabi powder if necessary.

Mix the two types of sesame seeds together and spread them out on a plate. Form the salmon mixture into 12–16 balls, each about 2 inches in diameter, packing each one firmly. Roll the balls in the sesame seed mixture and place them on the prepared baking pan.

Bake for 10 minutes, turning the pan around halfway through—the balls should begin to brown on the top. Keep an eye on them to make sure they don't burn underneath.

Serve with Citrus Ponzu dipping sauce (see page 113).

Shrimp Balls

Depending on who you are feeding, you can make a few variations to these balls. I love them with the pork added for an extra level of flavor and juiciness, but they are super tasty just made with shrimp if you have a "I don't eat meat but I do eat fish/shellfish" guest for dinner.

¾lb cooked shrimp, deveined and washed (½lb if combining with meat)

3½oz boneless pork shoulder or boneless, skinless chicken thighs, ground (optional)

1 free-range egg, beaten

2 tablespoon cornstarch

¾ cup Japanese panko breadcrumbs

2 scallions or 2 shallots, minced

2 garlic cloves, crushed

1 teaspoon sesame oil

2 teaspoons rice wine vinegar

1 tablespoon fish sauce

1 x 1-inch piece of fresh ginger, peeled and grated

¼ teaspoon freshly ground black pepper

salt to taste

Japanese panko breadcrumbs, for coating (optional)

sunflower oil for frying

Drain the shrimp and pat dry, then blitz them briefly in a food processor so they are roughly chopped. Add the ground pork or chicken (if using), egg, cornstarch, and breadcrumbs and blitz again, so everything comes together.

Transfer the mixture to a large bowl, add the rest of the ingredients, apart from the coating crumbs, and mix with your hands to combine. The mixture will be on the wet side but will firm up when chilled. However, if it seems too wet, add some more panko. Chill the mixture in the fridge for at least 30 minutes.

When you are ready to cook, wet your hands and form the mixture into 16 balls, each about 2 inches in diameter. At this stage, if you like, you can roll the balls in more of the panko breadcrumbs to give them a crisp, crunchy outside when fried.

Pour a good inch of oil into a deep skillet on medium-high heat. When the oil is hot and begins to shimmer, add the balls in batches and cook for 6 minutes, turning them after 2–3 minutes and heating the oil up again between batches. The balls should be golden brown and cooked through. Drain on paper towels before serving.

These balls are versatile. They're great on their own, with Cherry Tomato & Chile Jam (see page 108) or Nuoc Cham dipping sauce (see page 119). You could also go "Balls on the Line" style and skewer them after cooking. Or, for the complete meal, stir-fry some garlic and red chile in oil. Add some shiitake mushrooms, soy sauce, Chinese cooking wine, and bok choy or other greens, then drop in the cooked shrimp balls. Heat through and serve with steamed rice.

Serves
4–6

Tuna & Ginger Balls

These balls are best eaten on the day of cooking. The meaty tuna can stand up to the flavors of ginger and scallions. Try to get line-caught skipjack tuna, if possible, and don't overcook it. In fact, if your oven breaks down, just eat them raw.

1lb fresh tuna steak

1 large free-range egg

3 scallions, thinly sliced

2 garlic cloves, crushed

1 x 2-inch piece of fresh ginger, peeled and diced

2 tablespoons finely chopped cilantro

1 red chile, seeded and minced

1 tablespoon Dijon mustard

1 tablespoon soy sauce

zest and juice of 1 lime

1 cup breadcrumbs

1 teaspoon salt

½ teaspoon freshly ground black pepper

Preheat the oven to 425°F, and line a large baking pan with nonstick parchment paper.

Cut the tuna into 1-inch cubes and place it in the freezer for 20 minutes. Once chilled, pulse in a food processor. Be careful not to overprocess—you want to retain some pieces of fish for texture.

Beat the egg in a large mixing bowl. Add the tuna, scallions, garlic, ginger, cilantro, chile, Dijon mustard, soy sauce, lime zest and juice, breadcrumbs, salt, and pepper. Mix it all together with your hands until well combined.

Heat a small skillet over high heat. Break off a small amount of the mixture, flatten between your fingers, and fry until cooked. Taste to check the seasoning and add more if necessary. Cover the mixture and refrigerate for at least 30 minutes.

Form the mixture into 14–16 balls, each about 2 inches in diameter (wetting your hands will make the balls easier to shape). Place the balls on the prepared baking pan.

Bake for 10–12 minutes, turning the pan around halfway through—the balls should begin to brown on the top. I don't like to overcook tuna, as it's OK to eat it a little pink in the middle, so take a look at the balls after 8 minutes and decide how well done you want them to be. They are also good pan-fried in olive oil until browned all over.

These balls are great served in mini brioche slider buns, with arugula and garlic mayo (see Real Mayonnaise on page 115), or with a rice noodle salad with Pickled Carrot & Daikon (see page 148).

Serves
4–6

"Crab Ball-timore"

As a kid, heading to Whitsand Bay in Cornwall, in the far west of England, was a real treat. It was the local beach where Dad grew up, and his crabbing skills were Jedi-like. My brother and I would marvel as crabs were dislodged from their hiding places and put into our plastic buckets. Picking crabmeat without getting shell everywhere is tedious, but the sweet, soft meat is worth the work. The first references to "crab cakes" appeared in cookbooks from Baltimore, Maryland, in the early 1930s. These balls are inspired by those original recipes.

1 heaping tablespoon butter

3 scallions, thinly sliced, including green part

1 garlic clove, crushed

1 large free-range egg

2 tablespoons good mayonnaise

1 tablespoon chopped flat-leaf parsley

1 tablespoon chopped cilantro

1 teaspoon English mustard powder

2 teaspoons Worcestershire sauce

1 tablespoon paprika

1 lime, zest finely grated, then the lime cut into wedges

1 teaspoon salt

a pinch of cayenne pepper

1 cup breadcrumbs

1lb cooked crabmeat, white and brown

Japanese panko breadcrumbs, for coating (optional)

sunflower oil, for frying

Heat the butter in a large heavy skillet. Add the scallions and cook on low heat for 2 minutes, then add the garlic and cook on low heat for 3 more minutes, or until the white part of the onions is translucent and the green part soft. Remove from the heat and set aside to cool.

Beat the egg in a large mixing bowl, then add the mayonnaise, parsley, cilantro, mustard powder, Worcestershire sauce, paprika, lime zest, salt, and cayenne pepper. Finally, stir in the breadcrumbs, fold in the crabmeat, and add the cooled onions, scallions, and garlic. Mix everything together with your hands until well combined.

Heat a small skillet over high heat. Break off a small amount of the mixture, flatten between your fingers, and fry until cooked. Taste to check the seasoning and add more salt or cayenne if necessary. Form the mixture into 14–16 balls, each 2 inches in diameter, packing each one firmly. At this stage, if you like, you can roll the balls in panko breadcrumbs to give them a crisp, crunchy outside when fried.

To fry the crab balls, put 2 tablespoons of oil into a heavy skillet. Heat the oil on high heat until it shimmers, then cook the balls in batches for 6 minutes, turning them after 2–3 minutes and heating the oil up again between batches. The balls should be golden brown and cooked through. Drain on paper towels before serving.

Alternatively, you can bake the balls. Preheat the oven to 425°F, and line a baking pan with nonstick parchment paper. Put the balls on the prepared pan and bake for 12 minutes, turning the pan around halfway through—they should begin to brown on the top. Keep an eye on them to make sure they don't burn underneath.

Try serving these balls each on top of a single baby gem lettuce leaf, with some Chipotle Mayonnaise (see page 115) and a wedge of lime or lemon.

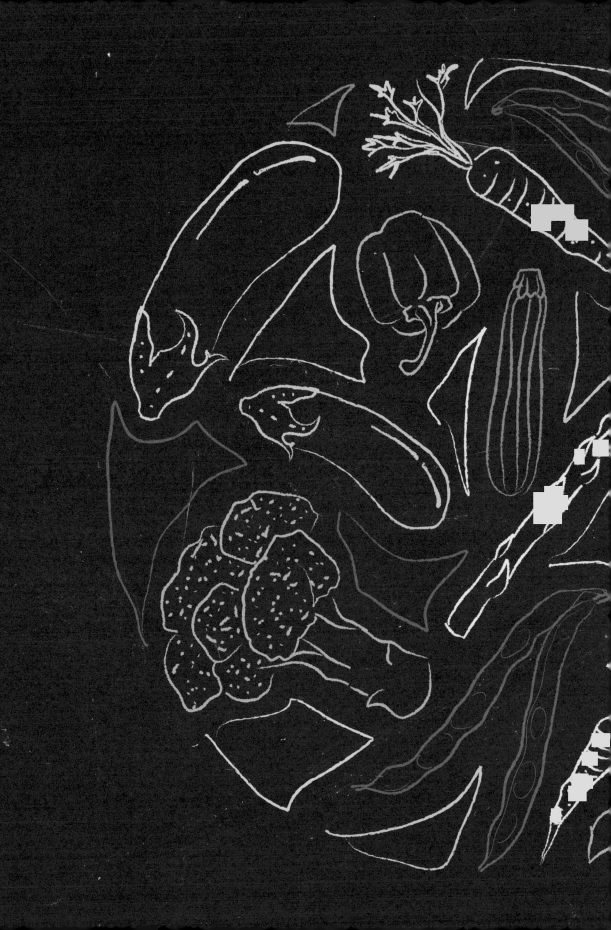

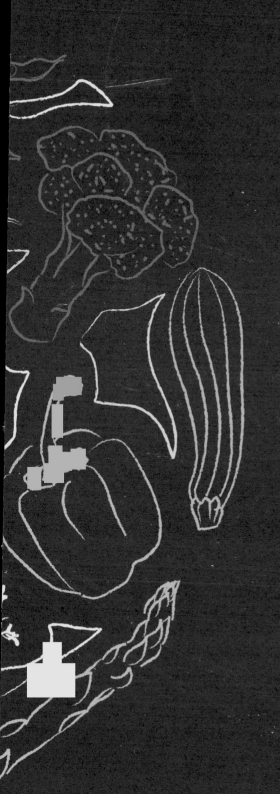

Serves
4

Brown Rice & Red Lentil Balls

These super-healthy balls contain all you need to get a low-fat, nutritious hit of fiber, protein, and minerals. Try getting the kids to eat a few. You can convince them it's all part of the fun after they have shaped and baked them with you.

½ cup red lentils

olive oil

3 shallots, thinly sliced

2 scallions, thinly sliced

1 garlic clove, crushed

1 cup pine nuts, toasted

1½ cups cooked brown rice, cooled

2 teaspoons thyme, finely chopped

2 tablespoons basil, finely chopped

zest and juice of 1 lemon

1 large free-range egg

1 cup breadcrumbs

1 teaspoon salt

½ teaspoon freshly ground black pepper

Preheat the oven to 425°F, and line a large baking pan with nonstick parchment paper.

Bring a pan of salted water to a boil. Add the lentils and bring back to a boil. Skim off any white foamy starch that rises to the surface. Cook for 5 minutes, or until the lentils are soft but haven't yet started to disintegrate. Drain in a strainer and leave to cool.

Meanwhile, heat a little olive oil in a skillet and add the shallots and the white part of the scallions. Stir-fry over medium heat for 2 minutes, then add the garlic and cook until the onions are translucent.

Place the toasted pine nuts in a clean dish towel and bash them with the back of a wooden spoon to break them (don't go too crazy, though, as you want to retain a few lumps for texture).

Beat the egg in a large bowl, then add all the other ingredients and mix with your hands until well combined. Form the mixture into 16 balls, each 2 inches in diameter, packing each one firmly, and place them on the prepared baking pan.

Bake the balls for 15–20 minutes, turning the pan around halfway through—the balls should begin to brown on top. Keep an eye on them to make sure they don't burn underneath.

Serve with Lowry & Baker's Belgian Endive, Stilton, Pear & Pecan Salad (see page 136), or with Simple Tomato Sauce (see page 99) along with a green salad.

Serves
4–6

Balafel

This is my nod to falafel, the popular Middle Eastern dish. Dried chickpeas are really easy to prepare and cook, the benefit being that you can control how soft to cook them, which helps if you want them to take a salad dressing or add texture. Always good to have a couple of cans tucked away though.

½lb fresh spinach, washed

2 tablespoons olive oil

4 shallots, finely diced

2 garlic cloves, crushed

2 teaspoons cumin seeds

1 teaspoons coriander seeds

1lb dried chickpeas, cooked
(see method on page 142)
or 2 x 15oz cans chickpeas, drained

½ teaspoon dried red pepper flakes

¼ teaspoon freshly ground nutmeg

2 teaspoons salt

¼ teaspoon black pepper

2 free-range eggs

7oz ricotta cheese

1½ cups breadcrumbs

1 tablespoon finely chopped
flat-leaf parsley

juice of 1 lemon

Preheat the oven to 425°F, and line a large baking pan with nonstick parchment paper.

Put the washed spinach, still wet, into a pan and add a splash of water. Cook over high heat, turning regularly, until the spinach has wilted and softened. Squeeze it between two plates to get rid of excess liquid, then chop finely.

Put the olive oil into a heavy skillet over medium heat. Add the shallots, garlic, and a sprinkling of salt and pepper. Stir-fry over low heat for 6 minutes, or until the shallots are translucent, being careful not to burn the garlic (add a splash more oil if things start sticking). Then add the spinach and stir frequently for a further 2 minutes. Leave to cool.

Heat a clean, heavy skillet over high heat and toast the cumin and coriander seeds for 2 minutes, moving them around in the pan so they don't burn. Then grind them in a mortar and pestle.

Put the cooked chickpeas into a food processor with the cumin and coriander seeds, dried red pepper flakes, nutmeg, salt, and pepper, and pulse to a rough paste with a chunky texture.

Beat the eggs in a large bowl and stir in the ricotta. Add the breadcrumbs, spinach mixture, chickpea mixture, parsley, and lemon juice. Mix everything together with your hands until well combined.

Heat a small skillet over high heat. Break off a small amount of the mixture, flatten between your fingers, and fry until cooked. Taste to check the seasoning and add more if necessary.

With wet hands, form the mixture into 20 balls, each about 2 inches in diameter, packing each one firmly, then place the balls on the prepared baking pan. Bake for 15–20 minutes, turning the pan around halfway through—the balls should begin to brown on the top. Make sure they don't burn underneath.

These are great served in toasted pitta bread with some Cumin Sour Cream (see page 111) or Spicy Lime Yogurt (see page 113).

Serves
3–4

Sweet Potato & Goat Cheese Balls

The sweet potato is a favorite of mine for vegetarian dishes. It has a great flavor and can be baked whole, or chopped and then deep-fried to make chips or fries. Kids love these colorful concoctions, and sweet potatoes also make a quirky side dish to go with roasted meats.

1¼lb sweet potatoes

½lb spinach, washed

1 free-range egg

1 heaped tablespoon butter

1 garlic clove, crushed

1 tablespoon lemon juice

1 tablespoon heavy cream

1¼ cups fresh breadcrumbs

2oz soft goat cheese

1 teaspoon finely chopped rosemary

1 teaspoon salt

1½oz Parmesan cheese, finely grated, or a good vegetarian Parmesan-style cheese

¾ cup Japanese panko breadcrumbs

freshly ground black pepper

Preheat the oven to 425°F, and line a large baking pan with nonstick parchment paper.

Place the sweet potatoes on a cookie sheet and bake for 40 minutes, or until the flesh is soft and can be easily pierced with a knife. Remove from the oven, allow to cool to the touch, then peel.

Put the washed spinach, still wet, into a large pan and add a splash of water. Cook over high heat, turning the spinach over regularly, until it has wilted and softened. Squeeze it between two plates to get rid of any excess liquid. Set it aside to cool slightly, then chop finely.

Mash the sweet potato in a large bowl with the egg, butter, garlic, lemon juice, and cream. Add the chopped spinach, fresh breadcrumbs, goat cheese, rosemary, salt, and a generous grinding of pepper. Mix everything together thoroughly using your hands. Place in the fridge for 30 minutes to an hour to chill and set a little. Depending on the water content of the potatoes, this can be quite a wet mixture, so add more breadcrumbs if you feel the balls won't hold their shape.

Mix the Parmesan and panko breadcrumbs together and spread them out on a flat dish. Take the vegetable mixture out of the fridge and form it into 14–15 balls, each about 2 inches in diameter. Roll the balls in the Parmesan and panko mixture and place them on the prepared baking pan.

Bake the balls for 15–20 minutes, turning the pan around halfway through, until the balls begin to brown on top. Keep an eye on them to make sure they don't burn underneath.

Great served with a baby leaf salad, toasted nuts, and some crisp pancetta.

Serves
4

Zucchini & Asparagus Balls

Grab some early-season zucchini and combine them with mid-season asparagus to make a tasty veg ball. It's important to remove as much liquid as possible from the grated zucchini to prevent sogginess and ball collapse. Simply wrap the grated zucchini in a clean dish towel and wring it out. Be careful when toasting the pine nuts—keep them moving around the skillet so they don't burn. I am the king of distraction here. Whole pans of pine nuts have ended up in the garbage can because I left them on the stove and forgot about them. You have been warned.

4 small zucchini

2 teaspoons sea salt

2 tablespoons pine nuts

2 free-range eggs

8 asparagus spears, sliced
and cut into paper-thin disks

2 garlic cloves, crushed

a large pinch of dried red pepper
flakes

1¼ cups fresh white breadcrumbs

¼ cup + 2 tablespoons finely grated
Parmesan cheese

3¼ cups Japanese panko
breadcrumbs

Coarsely grate the zucchini into a bowl and scatter with 1 teaspoon of the salt. Set aside for 20 minutes to draw out some of the liquid, then squeeze the zucchini in a clean dish towel. This is important, because you want to remove as much liquid as you can in order to help the mixture combine and stick together.

Put the pine nuts into a dry skillet and toast them over medium heat, shaking the pan from time to time and making sure they don't burn. Remove the pan from the heat as soon as they start to turn a light brown color and then tip them onto a cutting board. When they've cooled down, crush them into small pieces.

Beat the eggs in a large bowl. Add the asparagus, zucchini, garlic, dried red pepper flakes, white breadcrumbs, Parmesan, crushed pine nuts, and the remaining teaspoon of salt. Combine with a wooden spoon, then mix thoroughly using your hands, squeezing the mixture together as you go. The mixture will be fairly wet, so chill it into the fridge for 30 minutes to allow the flavors to infuse and the mixture to set.

Meanwhile, preheat the oven to 400°F, and line a large baking pan with nonstick parchment paper.

Pour the panko breadcrumbs into a shallow bowl. Form the zucchini mixture into 12 balls, each about 1¾ inches diameter, then roll them in the panko breadcrumbs and place them on the prepared baking pan. Bake in the oven for 15–20 minutes, turning the pan around halfway through—the balls should begin to brown on the top and be firm to touch. Keep an eye on them to make sure they don't burn underneath.

Delicious served with Cheese Sauce (see page 103) and fresh pasta, with a poached egg on top.

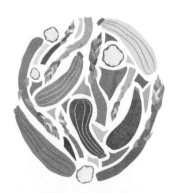

Balls 'n' Brews

When you are at a pop-up event you need a drink. A good bar takes a food market to the next level, and independent, artisan, craft brewers are on the rise. This is great news, as I am a big fan of hoppy pale ales and, in the past, the most readily available have been U.S. imports. On trips to the American West Coast I've been surprised to see so many artisan breweries passionately sculpting ales from home-grown hops so, for me, it's great to see there are now plenty of British options, too. At the markets there have been regular ball-for-brew swaps. This cooperation has recently extended further, with the Camden Town Brewery hosting Street Feast, one of London's most high-profile night markets, bringing the food right into the beers' backyard.

Andrew Cooper, accredited beer sommelier and founder of craft brewery The Wild Beer Co., is a big fan of pop-up event bars. It's a great way to get his brand out there to a core group of consumers who are passionate about what they eat and drink. Flavorful craft beers also lend themselves to pairing with food, with balls and brews having some great combinations. Here are Andrew's tips on which brews he thinks would best partner a few of my balls.

Beef & Chorizo Balls ~ Moor Illusion (Moor Beer Co.) A black IPA (India Pale Ale) is a great complement to these balls; earthy malt flavors work with the beef and juicy hops accentuate the spices in the chorizo.

Lamb, Rosemary & Garlic Meatballs ~ Modus Operandi (The Wild Beer Co.) Old English Ale aged for 90 days in oak barrels with wild yeast to produce a beer that is rich and fruity, with sweet cherries and tannins to complement the lamb.

Ballafel ~ Camden Pale (Camden Town Brewery) Punchy U.S. hops throw out big aromas and flavors of grapefruit, orange, and tropical fruit, which refresh the palate ready for the next bite.

Great Balls of Fire ~ Cannonball (Magic Rock Brewing Co.) Spices and hops are fabulous together. This hoppy IPA has plenty of bitterness, which nullifies the pungency of the spices, letting the hops and spices work together in a tongue-tingling taste sensation.

Crab Ball-timore ~ Fresh (The Wild Beer Co.) The freshest New World hops, with stunning tropical fruit flavors, possess just a little bitterness meaning that they won't overpower the delicate crab. Irresistible.

Smokin' Bacon Balls ~ Export India Porter (Kernel Brewery) The dark and roasted flavors here are the perfect partner to the beef and bacon balls, with the balancing hop presence in Kernel's masterpiece cleansing the palate of the delicious rich food.

Green Chile Chicken ~ Bristol Hefe (Bristol Beer Factory) Light and spritzy with banana, citrus zest, grapefruit, and spices that contrast and refresh the palate against the Thai chile flavors.

Game Balls-Ball Game ~ Bliss (The Wild Beer Co.) A Belgian farmhouse-style beer brewed with a blend of spices, roasted apricots, and a wild yeast; beautifully refreshing, wildly different, perfect with game.

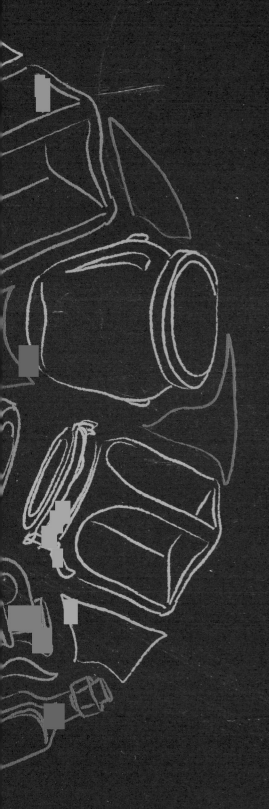

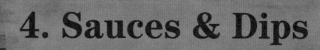

Red Wine Gravy

This one is going to come in handy whether you are serving it over a number of the balls in this book, high-quality sausages and mashed potatoes, or with roasted meat.

2 tablespoons olive oil

5 shallots, sliced

1 garlic clove, crushed

1 sprig of rosemary

2 tablespoons red wine vinegar

1 tablespoon redcurrant jelly

1¾ cups red wine (Rioja works well)

1¾ cups chicken or lamb stock

1 heaped tablespoon butter

salt and freshly ground black pepper

Heat the olive oil in a heavy skillet over medium heat. Add the shallots and a couple of grindings of salt and pepper. Stir for 5 minutes, or until the shallots are soft and start to brown. Add the garlic and rosemary and cook for a further 3 minutes, stirring occasionally to prevent it from burning.

Stir in the red wine vinegar and redcurrant jelly, which should bubble up and reduce fairly quickly to a syrupy consistency. Now add the red wine and let it reduce by half before adding the stock. Simmer until the mixture has reduced by two-thirds, then pour the sauce through a fine-mesh strainer, discarding the rosemary sprig.

Return the sauce to the pan, check the seasoning, and add more salt if required. Finally, stir in the butter to give the sauce a nice sheen. Great served with Lamb, Rosemary & Garlic Meatballs (see page 60).

Chicken Stock

Fresh chicken stock is easy to make if you remember not to throw away the roast-chicken leftovers. Simply use the stockpot method here, or freeze the carcass until a later date when you have a few more of them to make a bumper batch. You can ask your butcher for chicken carcasses if you want to get your hands on some quickly.

3 chicken carcasses, raw or cooked

1 onion, sliced

1 carrot, sliced

1 celery stalk, sliced

1 leek, sliced

a few sprigs of parsley

a sprig of thyme

1 bayleaf, torn

6 white peppercorns

Remove any excess fat from the chicken, then place all the ingredients in a stockpot or Dutch oven big enough to hold everything. Fill the pot with enough water to just cover the carcass, about 6 pints.

Bring to a simmer and skim off any fat and foam that appear on the surface. Simmer on a very low heat for 3 hours, skimming regularly, then pour the liquid through a fine-mesh strainer. To increase the flavor of the stock, reduce it rapidly to half its original volume, or until it tastes right to you. Set it aside to cool.

You can keep reducing the stock down, then freeze the concentrated stock in ice cube trays. The cubes can then be diluted for use in smaller batches.

Wild Mushroom Sauce

This is a rich sauce, but you can thin it down with a little stock,
or use light cream, to make it a little less rich.

3½ tablespoons butter

2 tablespoons olive oil

6 shallots

½lb button mushrooms
or mushroom trimmings,
roughly chopped

1 head of garlic, cut in half
horizontally

4 sprigs of thyme

1 cup white wine

1½ cups chicken stock

1½ cups heavy cream

7oz mixed wild mushrooms, cleaned

1 tablespoon freshly squeezed
lemon juice

salt and freshly ground black pepper

Melt 1½ tablespoons of the butter with the oil in a heavy skillet. Thinly slice 3 of the shallots and add them to the skillet, along with the button mushrooms/mushroom trimmings, garlic, thyme, and salt. Cook gently for 15–20 minutes, stirring occasionally to prevent the mixture from sticking to the skillet, until you have a soft, mushy, caramelized mixture.

Add the wine and let it simmer until reduced by two-thirds to a syrupy consistency. Add the chicken stock and simmer until reduced by half, then add the cream. Keep simmering, letting the sauce reduce by half again so that you get a nice thick consistency that coats the back of a spoon. Season to taste, then strain the sauce through a conical strainer, crushing and pushing all the tasty bits through with the back of a spoon or ladle.

Mince the remaining 3 shallots. Melt the remaining butter in a large deep-sided skillet until it foams, then add the shallots, stirring for 5 minutes until they start to soften.

Add the wild mushrooms and cook slowly until the liquid they give off has evaporated. Add half the lemon juice and stir.

Stir in the strained sauce and heat it through. Once it is simmering, add the last of the lemon juice, then check the seasoning and serve.

Barbecue Sauce

I use this as the base for the Honey & Garlic Sticky Ball Sauce (see page 96).
However, it's a versatile little number that can also be used for marinating chicken, pork,
or sausages prior to barbecuing, basting meat just before it comes off the coals, or just as a
dipping sauce. It gets even better after a few days mingling, once the flavors have got to know
one another. If you want a thinner sauce without the lumps of tomato, whizz it in a liquidizer.

2 tablespoons olive oil

1 small onion, minced

1 garlic clove, crushed

1 tablespoon tomato paste

1 x 14.5oz can of diced tomatoes

3 tablespoons apple cider vinegar

2 tablespoons tomato ketchup

2 tablespoons Worcestershire sauce

2 tablespoons pure honey

1 tablespoon Dijon mustard

1 tablespoon dark brown sugar

1 teaspoon sweet smoked paprika

½ teaspoon Tabasco

juice of 1 lemon

salt and freshly ground black pepper

Heat the oil in a heavy saucepan. Add the onion and cook on low heat for
2 minutes. Add the garlic and cook for another 3 minutes, or until the onion
is soft and translucent. Then add the tomato paste and stir for 3 minutes.

Now add all the other ingredients, apart from the salt and pepper, and
bring to a boil. Simmer for 15 minutes.

Season to taste and, if possible, leave to rest for an hour before using.
This sauce is even better if left for a day before using in the Sticky Ball
Sauce, because this allows time for the flavors to really develop.

Honey & Garlic Sticky Ball Sauce

This sauce uses my homemade Barbecue Sauce as a base (see page 95).
Honey and garlic may, at first, seem like an unlikely combination,
but go with it— it works really well.

1 tablespoon olive oil

5 garlic cloves, crushed

¼ cup + 1 tablespoon mild liquid honey

1 tablespoon soy sauce

1 cup Barbecue Sauce
(see page 95), or your favorite
ready-made version

½ cup tomato passata

Heat the olive oil in a medium-sized skillet over medium heat. Add the garlic and cook over low heat for 2 minutes, then add the rest of the ingredients and bring to a simmer. Cook, stirring frequently, for a further 3 minutes.

Use it in Sticky Balls (see page 33) or as a dip.

Chipotle Tomato Sauce

The chipotle chile is a smoke-dried jalapeño commonly used in Mexican cooking. It is great added to mayonnaise or used in a barbecue marinade, Here, it gives this tomato sauce a rich smoky flavor, perfect for Burritos (see page 22).

3 tablespoons extra virgin olive oil

3 red onions, thinly sliced

2 medium red chiles, seeded andminced

2 garlic cloves, crushed

3 tablespoons finely chopped cilantro stalks

2 tablespoons Bowler's Dry Spice Blend (see page 122)

1 tablespoon tomato paste

2 x 14.5oz cans of Italian diced tomatoes

1¾ cups Chicken Stock (see page 90)

1½–2 tablespoons soft light brown sugar

2 tablespoons chipotles in adobo sauce

juice of 1–2 limes

salt and freshly ground black pepper

Heat the olive oil in a wide deep skillet. Add the onions, cover with a lid, and cook gently for 10 minutes, or until very soft but not browned. At this stage, I would always add a few pinches of salt and grindings of pepper so the onions are seasoned from the start, meaning that you don't have to add so much later in the recipe.

Add the chiles, garlic, cilantro, and Bowler's Dry Spice Blend and stir for 5 minutes, or until the chiles have started to soften, making sure the mixture doesn't stick to the bottom of the skillet and burn. Add the tomato paste and cook for 3 minutes, again stirring so that it doesn't stick. Add the canned tomatoes, chicken stock, and a few pinches of salt. Bring to a boil, then simmer for 20 minutes, stirring occasionally to keep it from sticking.

Add 1½ tablespoons of the sugar, followed by 2 teaspoons of salt and the chipotles in adobo sauce. Stir and simmer for another 30 minutes, then taste. Add the remaining if necessary—the sweetness can vary depending on the flavor of the tomatoes. Add the lime juice at the end, to keep the freshness. You should now have a thick, rich smoky sauce. Adjust the seasoning, adding more salt or chiles as necessary.

Simple Tomato Sauce

I'm a big fan of all things spicy, but some occasions call for toning it down. Not a lot goes with a meatball better than pasta, Parmesan, and a thick, slow-cooked tomato sauce, great for kids and adults alike. Of course, if you can't face life without a little heat, just drop in a chile.

2 tablespoons olive oil

3 garlic cloves, halved

1 onion, minced

3 x 14.5oz cans tomatoes or good-quality Italian plum tomatoes, drained, juice reserved

½ teaspoon dried oregano

sugar, to taste

salt and freshly ground black pepper

Heat the oil in a heavy saucepan over medium heat. Add the garlic and cook for 2 minutes, or until it begins to turn golden, then add the onion and a pinch of salt. Turn down the heat and cook gently for 3 minutes.

Add the tomatoes and oregano and cook slowly. Break up the tomatoes with a wooden spoon after a couple of minutes. If it looks like it's sticking, add a little of the tomato juice.

Slowly cook this out for 1 hour, uncovered, then season to taste with salt, pepper, and a pinch or two of sugar if the tomatoes aren't singing with sweetness by themselves. You can serve the sauce before the hour is up if you are short of time, but it won't be as thick or rich.

Serve with any number of meatballs, or just as it is with some fresh pasta.

Spiced Red Onion & Tomato Sauce

When I'm asked what gives this sauce its flavor, I simply say, "I just get all the spices you can buy whole, toast them, grind them, and put them into the sauce." Although this is a slight exaggeration, it's pretty much the case. Be sure to take your time with this sauce, making sure the onions cook down slowly, then let the sauce reduce to get a rich flavor.

3 tablespoons extra virgin olive oil

3 onions, thinly sliced

1 x 2-inch piece of fresh ginger, peeled and diced

3 medium red chiles, seeded and thinly sliced

2 garlic cloves, crushed

3 tablespoons finely chopped cilantro stalks

2 tablespoons Bowler's Dry Spice Blend (see page 122)

1 tablespoon tomato paste

2 x 14.5oz cans of Italian or high-quality diced tomatoes

1¾ cups Chicken Stock (see page 90)

1½–2 tablespoons soft light brown sugar

3 tablespoons soy sauce

½ cup dried cranberries or raisins

juice of 1 lime

salt and freshly ground black pepper

Heat the olive oil in a large, deep skillet over low–medium heat and add the onions. At this stage, I would always add a few pinches of salt and several grinds of pepper so that the onions are seasoned from the start, meaning that you won't have to add so much later in the recipe. Give them a stir, then cover. Leave to cook gently for 10 minutes, or until very soft but not browned.

Add the ginger, chiles, garlic, cilantro stalks, and Bowler's Dry Spice Blend. Stir for 4 minutes, or until the chiles start to soften, making sure nothing sticks to the bottom of the skillet and burns. Then stir in the tomato paste and cook for 3 minutes, stirring all the time.

Add the diced tomatoes, chicken stock, and a few pinches of salt. Bring to a boil, then simmer for 30 minutes, stirring occasionally to prevent the sauce from sticking.

Add 1½ tablespoons of the sugar, the soy sauce, and the dried fruit. Stir and simmer for a further 15 minutes, then taste. The sweetness of the sauce can vary depending on the flavor of the tomatoes, so add more sugar or soy sauce as necessary. Taste again and add some or all of the lime juice. You should now have a thick, rich sauce that has a deep, sweet and sour flavor with warmth from the chiles and spices.

Best served with Great Balls of Fire (see page 34).

Crispy Cream

Crispy Cream, named after my aforementioned pal Crispin, who went to Sweden for a lady, is my take on the Swedish cream sauce that goes particularly well with the Björn Balls (see page 46). It uses a basic roux—a thickener made by combining flour and butter. You can make a batch and store it in the fridge for up to 2 weeks, so it's on hand for dropping into gravies and sauces.

2 tablespoons butter

2 tablespoons all-purpose flour

juice of 1 lemon

2½ cups beef stock

**1 tablespoon lingonberry jam
or cranberry jam**

½ cup heavy cream or sour cream

salt and freshly ground black pepper

Heat the butter in a large heavy pan. Add the flour and stir for 2 minutes to cook out the raw flour flavor, making a roux. Turn up the heat and add the lemon juice and the stock gradually, stirring constantly as you go, so the roux gets incorporated. Stir in the jam, which will make the sauce go a creamy orange color. Once the liquid reaches boiling point, turn the heat down and add the cream. Simmer the sauce for 20 minutes, uncovered, to reduce it, until it thickens enough to coat the back of a spoon.

Add the chilled Björn Balls to the sauce, cover, and cook for 20 minutes, turning the balls occasionally until warmed through. If the sauce gets a little too thick, add more stock. Adjust the seasoning and serve.

Blue Cheese Sauce

Blue cheese loves beef so this cold dipping sauce can really come in handy. I love it with Ball Shiitake (see page 27), and it makes a great dressing for salads, too.

1 small garlic clove, crushed

½ cup mayonnaise

½ cup sour cream

**2½oz blue cheese, such as Stilton,
Gorgonzola, or Roquefort,
finely crumbled**

1 tablespoon white wine vinegar

**1 tablespoon chopped chives or
green scallion tops**

salt and freshly ground black pepper

Put all the ingredients into a bowl and whisk until smooth.

Transfer to a jam jar, seal with a lid, and store in the fridge. It will keep for up to 4 days.

Preparation time **10** minutes Cooking time **10** minutes Serves **4–6**

Cheese Sauce

This is a universal sauce that works in a lot of combinations, so do experiment with it. It's the perfect accompaniment to pasta, polenta, and naked balls on a salad. I served this the very first time I got my balls out in public at a pop-up night, on top of Zucchini & Asparagus Balls (see page 84).

¼ cup butter

½ cup all-purpose flour

2½ cups milk

1¾ cups heavy cream

1 garlic clove, left unpeeled, squashed with the flat side of a knife blade

1 bay leaf

2 teaspoons salt

3oz Parmesan or Gruyère cheese, freshly grated

freshly ground black pepper

Heat the butter in a large heavy pan. Add all the flour and stir for a couple of minutes to cook out the raw flour flavor. Gently whisk in the milk and cream, and add the garlic, bay leaf, and salt. Stir continuously, until the liquid comes up to boiling point and starts to thicken. Simmer on the lowest heat setting for 5 minutes, stirring continuously.

Stir in the cheese until it has melted, and add a good few grindings of black pepper. Check the seasoning, and fans of cheese had better check the cheesiness (add a little more if the mood takes you).

Take the pan off the heat. Fish out and discard the garlic clove and bay leaf. If you are not serving this immediately, cover the surface with plastic wrap so that a skin doesn't form. Fresh herbs, such as parsley and thyme, can also be chopped and added to this sauce.

Guacamole

Guacamole is a key element of the Luardos burrito that's also perfect in other combinations. It's straight out of a Mexican cooking school in Oaxaca, where all the crushing and mixing was done with a mortar and pestle. We pair it up with our balls, so we like to keep it chunky—don't go too mad with the processor/fork/pestle. It's absolutely crucial the avocados are ones with a rich, creamy texture. If they're not, it's probably not worth making.

4 ripe Hass avocados

1 tablespoon extra virgin olive oil

3 tablespoons lime juice

½ a garlic clove, crushed

¼ of a jalapeño chile, minced

1 tablespoon chopped cilantro

½ a large red onion, minced

1 ripe tomato, seeded and diced

sea salt and freshly ground pepper

Scoop the avocado flesh into a bowl and roughly mash. Mix in the remaining ingredients and season with salt and pepper to taste.

I lather this in Luardos Meatball Burritos (see page 22), but it's also amazing used as a dip with Smokin' Bacon Balls (see page 41) and alongside our salads.

Tomato Salsa aka Pico de Gallo

Here's a tomato salsa recipe from our friends Luardos. It is a very simple fresh salsa and is absolutely crucial in the making of a good Burrito (see page 22). It's important to get the balance between sweet (sugar) and sour (lime) right. This will depend slightly on the ripeness of the tomatoes, so a little adjustment is sometimes required.

6 ripe tomatoes, cored, seeded, and finely diced

½ a Spanish onion, minced

½ a red onion, minced

1 tablespoon chopped cilantro

1 tablespoon extra virgin olive oil

1 bird's-eye chile, thinly sliced (optional)

a pinch of sea salt

3 tablespoons fresh lime juice

½ teaspoon superfine sugar

Put all the ingredients into a bowl and mix well. Give it a taste and add a little more lime juice and/or sugar if required.

Cover and set aside for 30 minutes to let the flavors combine.

Cherry Tomato & Chile Jam

I love chile jam and eat it on all sorts of things. I put this with the balls I serve with the Coconut Curry Sauce (see page 117), as the sweetness really works with the spices. I also whizz whole chiles in to add extra kick, but you can remove the seeds beforehand if you prefer. I always try a little bit of the raw chiles before I cook with them. The heat can vary from one chile to another, so a taste helps to determine how much or how little, seeds or no seeds, to go with.

2 garlic cloves, chopped

2 red chiles, chopped

1 x 1-inch piece of fresh ginger, grated

2 tablespoons fish sauce or soy sauce

1 teaspoon cumin seeds

2 teaspoons coriander seeds

¾lb cherry tomatoes, halved (or 14.5oz can of regular diced tomatoes)

½ cup red wine vinegar

1 cup golden superfine sugar

Place the garlic, chiles, ginger, and fish sauce into a food processor and pulse to form a paste.

Heat a heavy nonstick skillet over medium heat until it begins to smoke, then add the cumin and coriander seeds. Toast them for about 3 minutes, or until they begin to brown, start to pop, and give off a fragrant aroma. Remove them from the heat and grind them in a mortar and pestle.

Transfer the paste from the processor to a wide pan over medium heat. Add the tomatoes, vinegar, sugar, and ground spices. Turn up the heat and bring the mixture to a boil. Turn the heat down and simmer for 30–45 minutes, stirring regularly until it thickens to a jamlike consistency. When you draw a spoon through the mixture it should leave a line for a second. It will thicken up a little more when it cools, but definitely hold your nerve and don't pull the pan off the heat early.

Transfer the mixture into jam jars, seal with lids, and leave to cool. I sterilize jars by putting them into an oven heated to 300°F for 15 minutes and I soak the lids in boiling water for 5 minutes.

Serve with Green Chile Chicken Balls (see page 52), as a dip for Balls on the Line (see page 24), or even with a selection of your favorite cheeses.

Cumin Sour Cream

I use this on Great Balls of Fire, as it rounds off the dish well. It can make a tasty dip for raw veg and potato chips, too. For the best flavor I always recommend toasting whole cumin seeds and grinding them, but the ready-ground spice shortcut works too.

1 teaspoon cumin seeds

¾ cup sour cream

½ cup Greek-style yogurt

a pinch of cayenne pepper

1 small garlic clove, crushed (optional)

salt

Heat a heavy nonstick skillet over medium heat until it begins to smoke. Add the cumin seeds, shaking the pan constantly until they give off a nice aroma and begin to pop. Remove them from the heat, let them cool down a little, then grind them to a powder using a mortar and pestle.

Put the sour cream, yogurt, cayenne, and garlic (if using) into a bowl and add the ground cumin seeds. Give it a stir, add salt to taste, and serve.

❀ ❀ ❀ ❀ ❀ ❀ ❀ ❀

Preparation time: **15** minutes Cooking time: **2** minutes Makes **7**oz

Garam Masala

Garam masala is a spice blend that is used a lot in Indian cooking. "Garam" means hot and "masala" means spice. It's often added to dishes toward the end of cooking, and it's wise to add it little by little, as it can overpower dishes very easily. You can buy a ready-made mix if you're pressed for time. I use it to spice the Green Chile Chicken Balls (see page 52).

seeds from 30 green cardamom pods, husks removed

15 cloves

seeds from 5 black cardamom pods, husks removed

4 pieces of mace

4 x 1-inch sticks of cinnamon

5 tablespoons cumin seeds

2 tablespoons coriander seeds

1 teaspoon black peppercorns

Put a dry skillet over medium heat. Add all the spices, stirring continually to keep the seeds moving. After 1–2 minutes there will be an aroma as the seeds begin to release their oils. Once this happens, remove the skillet from the heat, pour the spices onto a plate, and leave them to cool.

If you're using an electric grinder or processor, wait until the spices are cool to the touch, then grind. Alternatively, use a mortar and pestle and grind to a fine powder by hand.

Allow to cool completely, then store in an airtight container. As long as the container is tightly closed after each use, the garam masala should last a long time. I like to make a fresh batch every 2 months.

Spicy Lime Yogurt

This tasty sauce and dip is cooling yet warming at the same time. You can add chopped
mint leaves instead of the cilantro, depending on what you might want to serve it with.
I like things spicy, so I'd advise adding half the lime juice and half the Tabasco recommended
here to start with, then adding the remainder to taste.

1 cup Greek-style yogurt

**2 tablespoons finely chopped
cilantro leaves**

finely grated zest and juice of 1 lime

1 teaspoon Tabasco sauce

1 tablespoon extra virgin olive oil

Simply mix the yogurt and cilantro together in a bowl with half the
lime juice and Tabasco. Taste, add more lime and Tabasco if necessary,
then beat in the oil.

Cover and refrigerate until ready to use. This would be nice with Baa Baa
Balls (see page 56) or Balafel (see page 81).

Citrus Ponzu

Ponzu is a Japanese sauce or dressing made by combining citrus juice and soy sauce.
The traditional citrus fruit used is called yuzu, but lime is much easier to find, so I'm using that.

juice of 1 lime

**1 tablespoon Japanese rice
wine vinegar**

2 tablespoons light soy sauce

1 teaspoon golden superfine sugar

1 teaspoon sesame oil

1 teaspoon mirin (optional)

zest of 1 lime

Put all the ingredients into a bowl and whisk until the sugar has dissolved.

This sauce gets better if it is refrigerated for a few hours or overnight,
to allow the flavors to mingle.

To make a dressing for salads, simply whisk the above sauce with
some sesame oil. You could go crazy and throw some sesame seeds
in there, too.

Chipotle Mayonnaise

This smoky-tasting mayo is great to use as a dip for fries, chicken, or fish, to spread on a sandwich (try it on a bacon, lettuce, and tomato sandwich), or a burger.

1 chipotle chile

¾ cup Real Mayonnaise (see below)

1 garlic clove, crushed

1 teaspoon adobe sauce

1 scallion, green parts only, thinly sliced

1 tablespoon fresh lime juice

sea salt flakes and freshly ground black pepper

Soak the chipotle chile in warm water for 15 minutes, then chop it finely.

Put all the ingredients into a large bowl, whisk together, and serve.

Real Mayonnaise

You need to be able to make your own mayonnaise so you can customize it with other ingredients and then slather it onto your buns, balls, and burgers. When you've done it once, and have seen how easy it is, there's no turning back. Just use a food processor. To save on wastage this recipe uses whole eggs; the whites help to stabilize the mixture. If you want a richer mayonnaise, add another egg yolk, increase the oil, and adjust the other ingredients to taste. I use olive pomace oil because it's lighter than olive oil and less likely to overpower the mayonnaise with an olive taste, but you should experiment and mix oils together to achieve a taste you like.

2 free-range eggs

1 tablespoon Dijon mustard

1½ cups olive pomace oil, olive oil, sunflower oil, or a combination

1 tablespoon white wine vinegar, apple cider vinegar, or lemon juice

freshly ground salt and black pepper

Put the eggs, mustard, salt, and pepper into the bowl of a food processor and pulse briefly to combine.

With the motor running, drizzle the oil in, slowly to begin with and then faster, as the eggs and oil begin to emulsify. Once the mixture has thickened up, add the vinegar. Taste, and increase the mustard, vinegar, salt, and pepper to your liking. At this stage you can also add other ingredients, like some Confit Garlic (see page 155), cilantro or other herbs, chiles, and other spices.

Coconut Curry Sauce

This Thai-inspired sauce is delicious with Green Chile Chicken Balls (see page 52), but also works with Great Balls of Fire (see page 34). Thai food has very distinctive flavors—sweet, sour, hot, and salty—that work together and need to be balanced. In this recipe, sweetness comes from the jaggery and the coconut milk, sourness from the limes, heat from the chiles, and saltiness from the fish sauce. Balance these to taste, and add the customary Thai basil and slivers of kaffir lime leaf for an authentic finish.

THE PASTE

1 tablespoon coriander seeds

1 tablespoon cumin seeds

10 fresh green Thai bird's-eye chiles, seeded and minced

2 shallots, diced

3 garlic cloves, roughly chopped

1 x 1¼-inch piece of fresh ginger, or galangal if you can find it

3 medium lemongrass stalks, tough ends and outer layer discarded, chopped

3 kaffir lime leaves

3 tablespoons chopped cilantro

1 teaspoon shrimp paste

1 teaspoon Thai fish sauce

½ teaspoon freshly ground black pepper

THE SAUCE

1 tablespoon peanut or vegetable oil

1 tablespoon paste (see above)

1¾ cup coconut milk

2 teaspoons jaggery

1 tablespoon Thai fish sauce

juice of 1 lime

2 kaffir lime leaves or zest of 1 lime

1 tablespoon Thai basil, chopped into slivers

Heat a heavy nonstick skillet over medium heat until it begins to smoke. Add the coriander and cumin seeds, shaking the pan constantly until they give off a nice aroma and begin to pop. Once this happens, remove from the heat and pour them onto a plate to cool. When the spices are cool, grind them to a powder using a mortar and pestle.

Put the rest of the paste ingredients into a food processor, add the ground seeds, and pulse to make a paste.

Heat the oil in a heavy pan over medium heat. Add 1 tablespoon of the paste and cook for 2 minutes, then add the coconut milk, stir to combine, and bring to a simmer.

Add the jaggery, fish sauce, lime juice, and lime leaves. Taste, and balance the sweet, sour, and salty flavors with a little more jaggery, lime, and fish sauce, if required. Simmer for 10 minutes, remove from the heat, stir in the Thai basil, and serve.

Peanut Sauce

Satay with attitude—great for dipping Green Chile Chicken Balls into (see page 52),
spreading on a piece of leftover naan bread, or, once chilled, using as a dip for raw veg.

2 tablespoons vegetable oil

1 small red onion, minced

1 small red chile, seeded and minced

1 garlic clove, crushed

generous ½ cup unsweetened coconut milk

3 tablespoons hot water

1 tablespoon dark soy sauce

¼ cup smooth peanut butter

¼ cup chopped roasted peanuts

1 tablespoon fresh lime juice

salt and freshly ground black pepper

Heat the oil in a medium pan. Add the onions and cook over low heat for
2 minutes. Add the chile and garlic and cook, stirring frequently, for a
further 3 minutes, or until the onion is soft.

Pour in the coconut milk and bring to a boil. Turn off the heat, add the hot
water and soy sauce, then whisk in the peanut butter. Stir in the chopped
peanuts and lime juice, and season the sauce with salt and pepper to taste.

Keep in a sealed jar in the fridge for up to 3–4 days. When it is chilled the
sauce will get thicker, so either use as a dip or soften it up in a pan over low
heat, adding a splash of water if necessary.

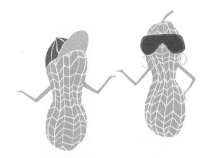

Nuoc Cham

This sauce is a staple in Vietnam. Primarily a dipping sauce for just about everything, it balances the sweet, sour, salty, and spicy elements that make Asian cooking so damn good and gives a nice flavor to the pork balls used in Vietnamese Noodle Soup (see page 18).

½ cup water

¼ cup granulated sugar

3 tablespoons freshly squeezed lime juice

1 tablespoon rice wine vinegar

2 small garlic cloves

2 red Thai chiles, seeded and minced

½ teaspoon salt

3 tablespoons fish sauce

Put the water, sugar, lime juice, and vinegar into a bowl and stir to dissolve the sugar. Taste to check the balance of sweet and sour, making adjustments if necessary.

Combine the garlic, chiles, and salt in a mortar and pestle and crush everything together to create a smooth paste.

Mix the garlic paste with the liquid in the bowl and add the fish sauce. Stir and taste again, checking the balance of sour, sweet, salt, and spice.

Pomegranate Seed & Cilantro Raita

Darina Allen's recipe, this refreshing raita will help cool you down when you've overspiced your balls. It is also a perfect accompaniment to the Ballymaloe Spicy Indian Meatballs (see page 59).

a large pinch of cumin seeds

1 pomegranate

1¼ cups plain natural yogurt

2–3 tablespoons coarsely chopped cilantro

salt and freshly ground pepper

Put the cumin seeds into a dry skillet and roast over high heat, shaking the pan frequently, for a minute, or until the seeds start to give off an aroma. Remove from the heat and set aside to cool.

Split the pomegranate in half around the equator, then hold one half, cut-side down, over a bowl. Tap vigorously with a wooden spoon. The seeds should dislodge and fall into the bowl. Repeat with the other half.

Stir in the yogurt, cilantro, and the freshly roasted cumin seeds, and season with salt and freshly ground pepper.

Serve with hot spicy dishes.

The Bowler's Dry Spice Blend

This is a great way to add some deep spice to your sauces and other cooking. It really pays to buy all these spices whole and toast them in a dry, nonstick heavy skillet. Once toasted, the spices can be ground in a mortar and pestle, coffee grinder, or food processor. The flavor you get from whole spices is much more intense and fresh than that of their ready-ground brothers, which will lose flavor once they hit the package and certainly once opened.

1 tablespoon fennel seeds

1 tablespoon coriander seeds

1 tablespoon cumin seeds

1 tablespoon fenugreek seeds

½ a star anise

1 whole cardamom pod

1 dried bay leaf

1 x 1½-inch stick of cinnamon, broken

¼ teaspoon ground nutmeg

1 tablespoon black or yellow mustard seeds

½ teaspoon nigella seeds

Heat a heavy nonstick skillet over medium heat until it starts to smoke.

Add all the ingredients to the dry pan, except the mustard seeds and nigella seeds. Shake the pan every few seconds to keep the spices moving. After 1 minute add the mustard seeds and nigella seeds.

After a further minute there will be a nutty, fragrant aroma coming off the skillet, and the coriander seeds and fennel seeds will start to turn a red-brown color. Once this happens and the seeds begin to pop, remove the pan from the heat and tip the spices onto a plate to cool down. (If you leave them in the skillet they will continue to cook and will quickly burn.)

If using an electric grinder or processor, make sure the spices are cool to the touch before grinding in batches—if they are still hot they can give off a bit of moisture and stick to the sides of the machine. Alternatively, use a mortar and pestle and grind the spices to a fine powder by hand.

Once ground, you can keep this spice mix in an airtight container for up to 4 weeks. Use it in the Chipotle Tomato Sauce (see page 98), Spiced Red Onion & Tomato Sauce (see page 100), or try adding some to a meatball mixture or use to flavor couscous.

5. Sides

Preparation time **2** minutes Cooking time **1** hour Serves **6**

Cheesed, Charred & Herbed Polenta

Polenta is a great side for meatballs, as it sits perfectly under any sauce and mops up leftovers brilliantly. You can also pour it into a baking pan to about a ½-inch depth, set it aside to cool, then slice it up and chargrill or fry it with a little olive oil.

1¾ pints water
1 teaspoon salt
1½ cups coarse polenta
5 tablespoons butter
3oz Parmesan cheese, grated
freshly ground black or white pepper

Put the water and salt into a large pan and bring to a rolling boil. Use a measuring jug to pour the polenta in a slow stream into the water, whisking as you go. Continue to stir until it comes to a boil, burping bubbles up, then turn the heat down to low. Continue to cook it for up to an hour (40–45 minutes might be enough), stirring regularly.

If you make a big batch, doubling the recipe, you can pour half the polenta into a buttered baking pan at this stage, filling it to about a ½-inch depth. Leave it to chill. When it has set, slice it up, lightly brush both sides with olive oil, and either fry in a ridged grill pan over medium heat or cook it under a broiler preheated to medium. Grill or broil it for about 2–3 minutes on each side, or until golden brown and charred.

Whisk the butter, Parmesan, and some white or black pepper into the hot mixture, let the cheese melt, then taste and add more salt if necessary. At this point you could also whisk in some fresh chopped herbs, such as chives, thyme, or parsley, etc.

If the polenta becomes too thick you can thin it by stirring in some hot cream, milk, or water. Serve hot with balls of your choice and plenty of sauce.

Mash Up

Why do mashed potatoes taste so good when you go out to a restaurant? Because they are loaded with more butter and cream than you would ever believe you can put in at home, that's why. I won't do that here, but we will use a combination of milk and cream because I like my mashed potatoes soft. To lighten the calorie load you can lose the cream and increase the milk, or man up and lose the milk and increase the cream.

2lb round white, round red, or Yukon Gold potatoes

½ cup heavy cream

½ cup milk, optional (omit this if you prefer firmer mashed potatoes)

4 tablespoons butter

salt and freshly ground black pepper

Wash the potatoes and place them in a large heavy pan. Cover them with cold water, add a teaspoon of salt, and bring to a boil. Boil for approximately 20–30 minutes, or until they are soft and a fork can be inserted into them easily.

When the potatoes are not far off being ready, put the cream and milk into a pan and bring almost to boiling point.

Drain the potatoes and peel them as soon as they are cool enough to be handled. Then mash the flesh immediately, using a masher, fork, or potato ricer for a fine consistency. Add the hot cream and milk, and the butter, beat in quickly, then continue to mash until you have a very smooth consistency. Add a geneous amount of salt and some grindings of pepper to taste.

For Garlic Mash Up, beat in 6 Confit Garlic cloves and 3½ tablespoons Confit Garlic oil (see page 155) when adding the butter.

In spring, if you're keen on a little foraging, pick some wild garlic leaves, thinly slice, then add them to the cream and milk mixture as it heats up. Beat the mixture into the potatoes, as above.

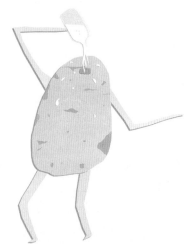

Potato Rösti

I love the mountains, and I try to escape there to ski, snowboard, and walk as often as I can. In Chamonix, in France, I always enjoy the creamy, cheese-laden, layered potato dish tartiflette, and in Switzerland I've always gone for slabs of rösti. Don't turn the rösti over too early—you want it deliciously crisp on the outside and soft in the middle. Try adding bits of bacon, cheese, and herbs to vary the dish.

2 tablespoons sunflower oil

1 small onion, diced

1½lb long white potatoes

4 tablespoons butter (or 2 tablespoons butter and 2 tablespoons goose fat)

salt and freshly ground black pepper

Heat the oil in a heavy skillet, then add the onion and cook for 5 minutes, or until the onion is soft and translucent but not browned.

Wash the potatoes, place them in a pan, and cover with cold, salted water. Bring to a boil, then cook for 5 minutes, or until just tender. Drain and peel when cool enough to handle. Chill for at least 3 hours—the cold air of the fridge helps dry the potatoes out and makes them easier to grate. If you are short of time you can omit this step, but the rösti might not be quite as crisp.

Grate the potatoes coarsely into a bowl, then add the onion and season with salt and pepper.

Melt 2 tablespoons of the butter in a heavy skillet. Add the potato mixture and flatten into a cake. Cook over low heat for 10 minutes, using a spatula to lift it occasionally to make sure the underside isn't burning.

Turn the rösti out onto a large plate. To do this, place your plate over the skillet, hold the plate down firmly, then flip both over. You will end up with the cooked side of the rösti facing upward on your plate. Melt the remaining butter in the pan and, once it is hot, slide the rösti back in, uncooked-side down, and cook for a further 5–10 minutes.

A lovely golden rösti makes the perfect side to many ball dishes, but I love it topped with a fried egg and some Smokin' Bacon Balls (see page 41).

The Pudding Bowler

Recently I wondered how I could make that British favorite, Yorkshire pudding, widely loved as a top comfort food, into the ULTIMATE comfort food? I decided to make the Yorkshire Puddings and fill them with more top comfort food. Double top! (See page 61 for the result).

2 free-range eggs

1 scant cup milk

scant ½ cup chilled water

1 cup all-purpose flour

a large pinch of salt

vegetable oil or beef dripping

Whisk the eggs, milk, and water together in a large bowl. Sift the flour and add it gently to the liquid, whisking as you go so that you don't get any lumps. The batter should come together and be nice and silky smooth.

Cover with plastic wrap and leave the batter for at least an hour to rest (in the fridge overnight is also fine). The longer the rest the higher the rise!

When you are ready to cook, preheat the oven to 425°F.

Take a Yorkshire Pudding pan with 3–4-inch diameter holes (a standard muffin or cornbread pan will also work) and fill each with ½ teaspoon of oil or beef dripping. Put the pan into the oven for 10 minutes to let the oil get nice and hot. Once hot, carefully pour in the batter two-thirds of the way up each hole. Bake them for about 20 minutes, or until they have risen and are golden brown.

To serve, fill each pudding bowl with a spoonful of mashed potatoes (any flavor you like) or some roasted baby new potatoes. Then choose your ball and ladle some sauce over it for the ultimate comfort food. I love the Lamb, Rosemary & Garlic Meatballs (see page 60) with Red Wine Gravy (see page 90), or the Veal & Parmesan Balls (see page 51) with Wild Mushroom Sauce (see page 92).

Puy Lentil Salad with Avocado, Halloumi & Walnuts

Lentils provide an earthy base for a number of salad and side variations. Cook them slowly, and always add the vinaigrette or dressing after draining the lentils but while they are still warm, as they absorb the flavor much better then. I've used slices of chargrilled halloumi here, but feta, goat cheese, or mozzarella all work well, too.

1 cup Puy lentils

a little olive oil, for frying

1 onion, sliced

1 garlic clove, crushed

1 large carrot, peeled and cut into large chunks

3 sprigs each of thyme and parsley

1 bay leaf

1 tablespoon olive oil

1 tablespoon apple cider vinegar

1 tablespoon soy sauce

2 tablespoons chopped flat-leaf parsley

½lb halloumi cheese, cut into ½-inch thick slices

2 tablespoons pomegranate molasses

2 tablespoons walnut oil

2 tablespoons extra virgin olive oil

1 romaine lettuce, cut into chunks

1 ripe avocado, sliced

¼ cup Caramelized Red Onions (see page 154)

3 tablespoons walnuts, roughly chopped

1 lime, cut into wedges

salt and freshly ground black pepper

Wash the lentils in cold water, then rinse and drain. Heat a little oil in a heavy pan. Add the onion and fry for 2 minutes, then add the garlic and cook gently until the onion begins to turn golden. Add the carrot, thyme, parsley sprigs, and bay leaf. Stir, then add the lentils and cover them with cold water.

Bring to a boil, then turn the heat down. Simmer for 20 minutes, or until the lentils have absorbed the water and are soft yet retain some bite. Add a little more boiling water if you need to. Remove the pan from the heat and drain the lentils, removing the carrot and herbs. Set the lentils aside for 5 minutes, then stir in the olive oil, vinegar, soy sauce, and chopped parsley. Taste for seasoning, remembering that the halloumi will be salty to taste.

Fry the halloumi slices in a dry pan or griddle them until they turn golden and soften.

Whisk together the pomegranate molasses, walnut oil, and extra virgin olive oil to make a dressing, and add a little salt and pepper.

Add the lettuce and avocado to the lentils, drizzle with half of the dressing, and toss everything together. Arrange on a platter or individual plates, with the halloumi and caramelized onions on top. Pour the rest of the dressing over everything, scatter with walnuts, then season and serve either warm or at room temperature.

This makes a great lunch on its own or with a side of Beef & Chorizo Balls (see page 28), Great Balls of Fire (see page 34), or Smokin' Bacon Balls (see page 41).

Lowry & Baker's Belgian Endive, Stilton, Pear & Pecan Salad

When I was developing the first few meatballs, and dreaming about balling in public,
I thought it would be a good idea to road-test a few recipes, but I needed a space.
Tucked away on Portobello Road in west London is a gem of a café called Lowry & Baker.
The owners, Katy and Maya, kindly agreed to give me the keys to their café for one night.
So, we popped up, rolled up, called it "Portoballo," and opened the doors to a few friends.
You can visit www.thebowleruk.tumblr.com/movies to get a flavor of the night and see the café.
This is one of Lowry & Baker's delicious salads, which makes a great side.

1 large handful of pecans, shelled

8oz mixed baby leaves (such as baby spinach, ruby chard, and wild arugula)

2 ripe pears

a squeeze of lemon juice

2 heads of red Belgian endive

7oz good-quality Stilton cheese (such as Colston Bassett)

¼ cup extra virgin olive oil

1 tablespoon white wine vinegar

1 teaspoon Dijon mustard

1 teaspoon real maple syrup

a pinch of salt and freshly ground black pepper

Heat the oven to 325°F.

Put the pecans on a baking pan and place them in the oven for about 10 minutes, or until you start to smell them toasting. Remove from the oven and allow to cool.

Place the baby leaves in a large mixing bowl. Cut the pears into quarters lengthwise and remove the core. Slice thinly lengthwise and add to the bowl. Squeeze a little lemon juice over them to stop them from discoloring.

Cut the Belgian endive widthwise, pull apart the leaves, and add to the bowl. Crumble in the Stilton, then add the toasted pecans.

For the dressing, combine the oil, vinegar, mustard, maple syrup, salt, and pepper in a jar. Screw the lid on securely and shake well to mix. Pour the dressing over the salad and toss everything together gently.

Divide between four nice plates and serve. I love it with Smokin' Bacon Balls (see page 41).

Jerusalem Artichoke Gratin

I love Jerusalem artichokes. They are a little secret weapon in my home cooking armory.
Not many people buy them, so when you use them to make soup, or a few fries, more
often than not you hit the target and people remark on the interesting flavor.
Here I've layered them alongside some potatoes in classic gratin style. This cooking
technique works with a lot of root vegetables, so feel free to experiment.

1 cup heavy cream

1 cup milk milk

1 garlic clove

juice of ½ a lemon

**¾lb round red or round white
potatoes, peeled**

¾lb Jerusalem artichokes, peeled

1 leek, sliced

2 tablespoons butter

**salt and freshly ground
black pepper**

Put the cream, milk, and the garlic clove into a large pan and bring to a
boil. Remove from the heat and set aside to cool, to allow the garlic to infuse.

Meanwhile, fill a bowl with cold water and add the lemon juice. Slice the
potatoes and artichokes into ⅛-inch rounds. Drop the slices of artichoke
into the bowl of lemon water as you go to stop them from discoloring.

Preheat the oven to 325°F.

Grease an ovenproof dish with a little of the butter and arrange a layer of
potato slices, slightly overlapping one another, in the bottom. Season with
salt and pepper, then add a layer of artichoke slices and season again.
Seasoning each layer as you go, scatter with leek slices, then add another
layer of artichokes and finish with a layer of potatoes. Fish the garlic clove
out of the milk and cream mixture and discard it. Then carefully pour the
mixture all over the gratin so that it just covers the last potato layer. Push
the top layer down gently. Dot the rest of the butter all over the top.

Bake in the oven for about 1 hour, or until golden brown and bubbling
around the edges. If the top looks like its browning too quickly, cover it
with a piece of foil to prevent it from burning.

I eat this gratin by itself, hot or cold. It also works well with a large number
of balls, especially Pork & Fennel Meatballs (see page 16), Ball Shiitake
(see page 27), and The Popeye (see page 36).

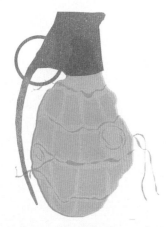

Nutty Bulgur Wheat Salad

Bulgur wheat is used to make tabbouleh, but is often overlooked as a tasty side.
You can combine a lot of ingredients with it to create a fresh-tasting salad to accompany
your favorite balls. Great with Beef & Chorizo Balls (see page 28) or at a barbecue with
skewered Balls on the Line (see page 24).

2 cups Chicken Stock (see page 90) or vegetable stock

1 garlic clove, peeled and squashed with the flat side of a knife blade

2 sprigs of thyme

1 cup bulgur wheat

1 tablespoon dried currants

¾ cup pecans, chopped (or walnuts)

1 red onion, thinly sliced

juice of 1 lemon

2 tablespoons olive oil

2 tablespoons chopped flat-leaf parsley

2 tablespoons chopped mint

sea salt flakes

Put the stock into a pan with the garlic and thyme. Bring to a boil, then reduce the heat and simmer for 2 minutes to let the flavors infuse a little.

Add the bulgur wheat and dried currants to a bowl. Now remove the garlic and thyme from the stock and pour it over the bulgur wheat. Let the wheat absorb the liquid for a few minutes while it cools a little. Stir in the pecan nuts, onion, lemon juice, olive oil, parsley, and mint.

Season with a couple of pinches of sea salt flakes and serve underneath your chosen balls with your favorite sauce and some peppery salad leaves.

Zucchini, Chickpea & Feta Salad

This is a great salad for barbecuers and ballers alike. It's hearty enough to make a standalone "meal in one" as well as being a good accompaniment to balls.

1 x 14oz can of chickpeas, drained, or ¼ cup dried chickpeas, soaked overnight

2 tablespoons olive oil

1 red onion, sliced

2 garlic cloves, crushed

1 red chile, seeded and sliced

1 teaspoons thyme leaves

zest and juice of 1 lime

7oz feta cheese

4 zucchini, green and yellow if possible

7oz baby leaf salad (such as watercress, spinach, ruby chard)

THE DRESSING

¼ cup Confit Garlic oil
(see page 155), or olive oil

2 tablespoons white wine vinegar

2 teaspoons honey

salt and freshly ground black pepper

If using soaked dried chickpeas, drain them, put them into a large pan, cover them with three times their volume of water, and bring to a boil. Simmer partially covered for 2 hours, testing after this time to see that they are soft but retain a little bite. Drain and allow to cool.

Heat the oil in a heavy skillet over medium heat. Add the red onion and cook on low for 2 minutes, then add the garlic, chile, thyme leaves, and a pinch of salt. Cook for another 4 minutes, or until the onion is soft and translucent, then add the chickpeas and cook on low heat for 5 minutes, stirring occasionally and adding the lime zest and half the juice for the last couple of minutes. Check the seasoning, crumble in the feta, and set aside to cool to room temperature.

Meanwhile, wash and dry the zucchini. Using a vegetable peeler, peel off strips of zucchini lengthwise down one side, coming in as close as you can to the central core, then turn and do the same to the other side. You should get strips with green or yellow skin on the edges.

Put a ridged grill pan over high heat. When it's hot, brush a few of the larger strips of zucchini with a little oil and arrange them lengthwise in the pan. Chargrill the zucchini strips on one side until you get grill marks, then turn them over and do the same on the other side.

Bring a pan of salted water to a boil, drop the remaining zucchini strips in for 1 minute, then drain and refresh under cold water.

Put all the dressing ingredients into a jam jar, secure with a lid, and shake vigorously to combine.

Put the baby leaves into a bowl and toss with a little of the dressing so they are lightly coated. Arrange the zucchini in a serving dish, put the baby leaves on top, and pile the chickpea and feta mix on top of that.

Serve with Baa Baa Balls (see page 56) for a double feta hit.

Preparation time **15** minutes, plus chilling Cooking time **none** Serves **4–6**

Spicy Slaw

I hate limp, acidic, carrot-laden coleslaw. It was served so often with baked potatoes at my school that it almost turned me off for life. However, if you up the quality of the ingredients and allow time to let the flavors combine, a side of coleslaw can give a lot of meatball dishes a bit of crunch. I suggest you make your own mayonnaise, though any type of mayo you have on hand will work. Feel free to substitute a different type of chile for the jalapeños.

¼ of a red cabbage, core removed

¼ of a white cabbage, core removed

1 teaspoon sugar

2 scallions, thinly sliced

1 tablespoon diced red jalapeño peppers (you can use the ones in a jar if you can't find fresh)

1 tablespoon finely chopped cilantro, leaves and stalks separated, plus a few extra leaves to garnish (optional)

¼ cup Real Mayonnaise (see page 115)

¼ cup sour cream

2 teaspoons wholegrain mustard

juice of ½ a lemon

2 teaspoons apple cider vinegar

1 teaspoon sea salt

½ teaspoon freshly ground black pepper

Thinly slice the cored cabbage quarters. You can use a mandoline slicer for this, but mind those fingers. Put the cabbage into a large bowl, sprinkle with the sugar, and stir well. Then add the scallions, jalapeños, and cilantro stalks, and mix everything together.

In a separate bowl whisk together the mayonnaise, sour cream, mustard, lemon juice, apple cider vinegar, salt, and pepper. Pour this dressing over the sliced cabbage mixture and toss gently to combine.

If you really have to tuck in immediately, go ahead, but I prefer to cover the bowl with plastic wrap and refrigerate it for 1–24 hours, to allow the flavors to mingle. Scatter with the cilantro leaves just before serving, if you like.

Citrus Couscous

This couscous is a meal in itself. Some people reckon couscous is bland, but I think it can be the backing band to a load of wonderful solo ingredients. This is great alongside the Baa Baa Balls (see page 56) and can be spiced up with some harissa.

¼ cup extra virgin olive oil

1 onion, minced

1 garlic clove, crushed

½ teaspoon dried red pepper flakes

1¼ cups couscous

2 cups boiling water

3 tablespoons pine nuts

seeds from 1 pomegranate

3 tablespoons finely chopped mint

3 tablespoons finely chopped flat-leaf parsley

juice of 1 orange

juice and finely grated zest of 1 lime

sea salt flakes and freshly ground black pepper

Heat the oil in a large heavy pan. Add the onion and cook on low heat for 2 minutes. Add the garlic and cook for a further 5 minutes, or until the onion is soft and translucent. Then add the dried red pepper flakes to the oil, stir, and set aside.

Put the couscous into a large bowl and stir in the boiling water. Add ½ teaspoon of salt, then cover the bowl with plastic wrap and set aside for 10 minutes.

Meanwhile, heat a dry skillet over medium heat and add the pine nuts. Toast them until they are golden, keeping them moving around the pan so they don't burn. Once toasted, put them into a bowl.

Split the pomegranate in half around the equator, then hold one half, cut-side down over a bowl and tap vigorously with the back of a wooden spoon. The seeds should dislodge and fall into the bowl. (Don't perform this near any new white carpets or curtains.)

Add the rest of the ingredients to the couscous and mix with a fork to fluff it up and separate the grains. Taste, adjust the seasoning, and serve.

Unless you're serving it with the Baa Baa Balls (see page 56), you can crumble in some feta or goat cheese, too.

Pickled Carrot & Daikon

A daikon, also called mooli, looks like a huge white carrot. This large Asian radish can
be eaten raw or cooked. It's great shredded and mixed with Citrus Ponzu (see page 113),
julienned, stir-fried, thrown into a curry, or pickled, as it is here.

½lb carrots

½lb daikon, woody bits removed

1 teaspoon salt

3 tablespoons superfine sugar

½ cup warm water

¾ cup rice vinegar

Julienne the carrot and daikon by slicing them thinly lengthwise, then
chopping them into matchsticks.

Dissolve the salt and sugar in the warm water. Stir in the vinegar. Put the
carrots and daikon into a jar and pour in the pickling liquor, making sure
the vegetables are covered. Seal the jar and refrigerate for at least an hour
before using. It's best eaten after 3 days, and will keep in the fridge for up
to 2 weeks.

Pickled Cucumber

This recipe gives the cucumber a sweet and sour taste, with a crunchy bite.
I use it as a relish when I serve my meatballs Bun 'n' Ball style (see page 29) in sliders
or alongside Björn Balls (see page 46).

¾ cup soft light brown sugar,
or golden granulated sugar

¾ cup apple cider vinegar, or white
wine vinegar

2 tablespoons salt

2 cucumbers, weighing about 1lb in
total—any more and the liquid won't
cover them, sliced into thin disks

4 shallots, sliced, or 1 large onion,
quartered and thinly sliced

Put the sugar, vinegar, and salt into a bowl and whisk together. Add the
cucumbers and shallots, stir, then cover the bowl and refrigerate for at
least 4 hours. Transfer to a sterilized jar—they will keep in the fridge for
up to 1–2 weeks.

Honey-roasted Vegetables

This is a simple way to cook vegetables, with the honey glaze enhancing their sweetness.
There are no real rules, just adjust the type of veg and the quantities and roast them the same
way. Don't overcook the veg, though—you should be able to insert a knife easily into them, but
at the same time they should retain a little bite.

**1 sweet potato, peeled, halved, and
cut into 1-inch chunks (you can use
butternut squash or pumpkin if you
prefer your veg less sweet)**

2 red onions, cut into 1-inch chunks

**1 red or yellow pepper, seeded and
cut into 1-inch squares**

**2 carrots, sliced diagonally
½ inch thick**

**2 zucchini, sliced diagonally
½ inch thick**

2 tablespoons olive oil

2 tablespoons liquid honey

leaves from 3 sprigs of thyme

¼ cup toasted pine nuts (optional)

**sea salt and freshly ground
black pepper**

Preheat the oven to 425°F.

Put all the vegetables into a roasting pan or ovenproof dish that can
accommodate them easily. Drizzle them with the olive oil and half the
honey, then scatter with the thyme, and season with salt and pepper.

Roast the veg for 12 minutes, then give them a shake, add the remaining
honey, and roast for a further 5–10 minutes. Remove from the oven and stir
in the pine nuts, if using.

These roasted veg are great with many of the balls in this book, especially
Lamb, Rosemary & Garlic Meatballs (see page 60), as well as alongside
roasts, or simply served on top of couscous with some goat cheese.

Asian Greens

"Always eat your greens!" we were constantly being told when we were little.
Now I can't get enough of them, cooked the Asian way with lots of chile, ginger, and garlic.
It's a great way to get more vegetables into your diet. They complement many of the
meatballs in this book, so they're the perfect green side.

1lb greens (a mixture of bok choy, purple sprouting broccoli, kai lan, and green beans)

1 tablespoon sunflower oil

1 teaspoon grated fresh ginger

1 green or red chile, seeded and thinly sliced

1 scallion, thinly sliced, green and white parts kept separate

1 garlic clove, crushed

1 tablespoon soy sauce

2 teaspoons sesame oil

Steam the vegetables over a pan of boiling water until just tender. Bok choy will take 2 minutes, sprouting broccoli, kai lan, and green beans will take up to 5 minutes.

Heat the sunflower oil in a wok or a large heavy skillet over high heat. Add the ginger, chile, and the white part of the scallion and stir-fry for 1 minute in the hot oil. Add the garlic, stirring constantly to make sure nothing sticks to the bottom of the pan and burns, then add the steamed greens and the soy sauce and toss gently to coat.

Add the sesame oil at the end and serve immediately, with the green part of the scallion scattered on top.

Caramelized Red Onions

This is a simple way to really enrich and intensify the flavor of red onions. I often make a large batch and keep them in the fridge, for adding to salads, omelets, burgers, and balls.

¼ cup olive oil (add 1 extra tablespoon if using the oven method)

¾lb red onions, sliced

2 tablespoons brown sugar (optional)

1 tablespoon balsamic vinegar (optional)

salt and freshly ground black pepper

STOVETOP METHOD

Heat the oil in a large heavy pan. Add the onions, along with a grinding of salt and pepper, and cook on low heat, stirring occasionally, for 30–45 minutes, or until they are golden brown and sticky in appearance.

You can substitute white onions for red, and add 2 tablespoons of brown sugar and 1 tablespoon of balsamic vinegar 10 minutes before the end of the cooking time if you like.

OVEN METHOD

To make larger quantities, you can spread the onions on a baking pan, cover them with the oil, sugar, vinegar, salt, and pepper, and bake at 325°F for 45 minutes, giving them a little stir halfway through, or until caramelized and sweet and sour to taste.

Crispy Fried Shallots

I sprinkle these crispy devils on top of the Green Chile Chicken Balls (see page 52), but they are a great garnish for many dishes. They keep well in a sealed jar.

6 shallots, thinly sliced

1 teaspoon salt

2 cups water

¼ cup vegetable oil

If you have time, it's a good idea to toss the shallots in the salt in a bowl, add the water, and leave for 30 minutes—it helps give them that extra crunch. If you are in a hurry, though, you can skip this step.

Pour the oil into a heavy skillet or wok over medium heat. Drain and rinse the shallots and dry them thoroughly. When the oil is hot, add the shallots and fry for 2–3 minutes, or until they turn golden brown and crispy. Watch them like a hawk because you want them to caramelize, not burn.

Take them out of the oil with a slotted spoon and drain on paper towels. Either use immediately or let them cool down, then transfer them to a clean jam jar to use at a later date.

Confit Garlic

Confit is a way of preserving most often associated with meats, in which they are cooked
in their own fat. Duck leg confit is the best-known example. Duck legs are cooked slowly
in duck fat and then allowed to cool, the fat enveloping the meat to preserve it.
Here I've slowly cooked garlic in oil, which makes the cloves tender and sweet,
with the oil becoming infused with garlic in the process.

**3 bulbs of garlic (about 30 cloves),
peeled, with the brown root end
trimmed off**

1 cup olive oil

There are two ways of doing this. The first is to put the garlic and oil into
a large heavy skillet into which the garlic will fit comfortably in one layer,
making sure it is completely covered by the oil. Heat the oil gently until
small bubbles start to form, then turn the heat down to low. You don't
want the oil to boil—this is all about low and slow—and you don't want to
brown the garlic. A simmer mat diffuser is good for this, to stop the oil from
getting too hot, otherwise you'll have to take the skillet off the heat every
time it looks as though it's getting hot enough for the garlic to brown.

Cook, checking regularly, for 30–60 minutes. You are aiming to get the
garlic to a soft consistency, so that you can pierce it easily with a knife
or squash it against the side of the pan.

The second way to confit the garlic is to heat the oven to 300°F. Get an
ovenproof dish, put a single layer of garlic in it, cover it with oil, and slowly
cook for 45 minutes to 1 hour until the garlic is soft, as described above.

Once the garlic is cooked, turn off the heat and let the pan or dish cool
down. Remove the cloves with a fork or a slotted spoon and put them into
a sterilized jar. Add the oil, seal with a lid, and refrigerate for up to 4 weeks
(you won't keep it that long, though, because it is too good not to use). The
oil is perfect for using in dressings and mayonnaise and for drizzling over
pizzas, and the cloves can be stirred into mashed potatoes and sauces.

Bean Balls

Surprise and apologies, but these balls aren't made from beans at all.
I met Bean Sopwith in an earlier life—she even lent me her apartment to do some meatball
preparation once. Whenever we're talking about food she's always suggesting ingredients and
alternatives to make things healthier, protein-enriched, and all round "superfoodier." Bean is
a nutrition and behavioral change expert, and she's kindly come up with a super-fuel snack
ball we can all make and eat on the go—in between meals, at school, or a couple of hours
before an exercise session. Get ready for a ballsy, health food hit.

**3½oz creamed coconut block
(for a healthier alternative,
use ¼ cup coconut oil plus a 1¼-inch
square of creamed coconut block
melted with a little hot water)**

**scant ½ cup organic nut butter
(the best is almond)**

**1 cup rolled oats (or use 1 cup
pumpkin seeds, soaked overnight,
for a low-carb alternative)**

**¼ cup jaggery (see * for alternative
healthier sweeteners)**

**½ cup desiccated coconut
(optional), plus extra for rolling**

¾ cup cocoa powder

1 teaspoon ground cinnamon

1 cup blueberries (optional)

2 teaspoons vanilla extract

Melt the coconut block (with the coconut oil, if using) in a pan over low heat. Then either process all the ingredients together in a food processor or mix them together by hand in a bowl.

Line a small shallow dish with parchment paper and roll the mixture into about 35 balls each about 1¼ inches in diameter. This can be a somewhat messy, so it's best to keep your hands cool by dipping them frequently into cold water. Pour some desiccated coconut onto a plate, then roll the balls in it to coat and place on a baking pan.

Freeze for 1 hour to harden the balls, then store in the fridge. These are best eaten straight from the fridge. As well as eating them on the go you can serve them with fresh blueberries, meringues, and some cream for an alternative dessert.

Now wow your friends with these facts from Bean: "These balls are better than most convenience snack foods because they contain healthy fats and proteins that don't overstimulate insulin production, and are therefore less likely to cause weight gain and will give a more consistent energy output. Four balls is a healthy meal replacement, which is especially useful if you are out on the road and healthy options are limited. If all gas stations sold these balls, there would be some happier, healthier travelers out there. Maybe we could even reduce some road rage with raw balls."

* Healthy sweeteners: Most supermarkets now stock natural sweeteners made from plant extracts, including xylitol (found in berries and fruit). Another natural sweetener is stevia, which is extracted from the plant of the same name. It is available in most health food stores in granules or as a liquid, and you can also buy it online. You can also use Zsweet, date syrup, maple syrup, or wild honey—all available at larger health food stores. There are many websites that sell these products online if your local health food store doesn't stock them. Avoid using agave—this is not a health food.

Index

Author's Acknowledgments

I feel incredibly lucky to have been given the opportunity to write this book. There are loads of people to thank, those who physically put the book together, but also all those that helped me get The Bowler to a place where a book was even a viable proposition. This list will be long, but it's important. Huge thanks and respect to all those who stand in line on cold, rainy February lunchtimes and all those who set up your stands, hours before the lunchtimes begin. Without your support, passion, and dedication this wouldn't have been possible.

Thank you to everyone at Smart Hospitality whose help on every level has been unfathomable. Robin Bidgood for listening at the start, and the pep talks along the way, Greg Lawson for his time and knowledge, and David Ridgway for his "calm under pressure" and "nothing's a problem" attitude—a true gent.

To head chef Rhys "Grhys-ball" Janzin for inspiration and passing on the tricks of the trade. Matthew Hughes, Jonny Hannan, Zoe Wager, Simon Read, Ryan Potter, and Richard Gee for putting up with, and answering, all my inane questions. Fabian, Dorothy, Nick, Leon, Rob, Tom, David, and everyone else, you know who you are. Seriously, when you're a lone ball slinger, seeing your friendly faces is a real boost and comfort.

Thanks to Gary Bentley, Lee, and everyone at the butchers, Bentleys of Surrey. Passion, knowledge, and knife skills. To allow me to work alongside you, and not make the tea, is truly generous.

Andy Ashton who gave me my first chance at being a baller back in 2011 and, when I tried to get out of it, forcing me to do the event. To Petra Barran of KERB (formally Eat.St) who is busy championing food on the streets as I write. Hannah Norris from Nourish PR for her insider industry knowledge and help with getting the book out there. Jonathan Downey for Tweat'ing up and supporting the scene. Ghislain Pascal for his no-nonsense advice, life support, and letting me loose in The Imperial Arms kitchen. Thanks to the marketeers who take on the spaces and take time to negotiate places for us to trade. Noticeably Toby Allen for setting up the wonderful Brockley Market and Dom Cools-Lartigue for night market, Street Feast London.

Algy Batten, Mark McConnachie, and the team at Fivefootsix. Not only did they kick my arse to get things going but their initial design and branding skills launched The Bowler. Thanks also for putting a roof over my head in years gone by.

My niece Nia Felwick, god-daughter Mathilda Douglas, and Ottilie Douglas for agreeing to demonstrate their rolling skills for the book. You're beautiful.

To Alison Starling at Octopus Publishing for literally getting the ball rolling, thinking there's a book in them balls and assembling a team to create something above and beyond expectation. To Sybella Stephens for editing and cracking the whip so I got everything in (almost on time), and Juliette Norsworthy for designing such a beautiful book. Catherine Phipps for helpful comments on my recipes and Annie Rigg for making a series of spheres look so different. Abigail Read whose ball-point pen and pencil skills produced the beautiful and quirky illustrations. Cris Barnett, your genius photography speaks for itself. Thank you for taking the project on—you're the best vegetarian option I've come across.

Thanks also to Dan Stephings, Jim Greayer, Chris McIntosh, Toby Allen, Louis Fernando, Andrew Ager, and Roberto Ruiz (ruizherrera.com) for the addional photography on the endpapers.

To my friends who have stuck with me over the years. You know who you are. I'm very lucky to have such an amazing group of brothers and sisters, and genuinely, without your support, encouragement, and help The Bowler would not be rolling.

Shouts go out to the ballers. Those of you who have been baptized in spicy tomato sauce and helped to sell. Bertie "my balls, your mouth, five pounds" Ager, Matthew "Kiwi Matt" Goodwin, and Jim "nice Swedish meatball snaps" Greayer. Dan Stephings for both balling and last-minute design and photography and Gavin Douglas for his cabbage slicing on Eat.St and the rest.

A special mention for Daniel Johnson-Allen who gave up his weekends in the early days to make sure I got settled. I cannot thank you enough.

And the family: Mum and Dad, you are an inspiration, full of life, love, and passion. Your support for everything I've ever done, and the stable home you created for us, provides a strong base, where jumping into something new becomes easier, knowing whatever happens there will be a hug, cuppa, slice, and kind words, ready to comfort. My brother Matt and little sis (in-law) Siân. Clever, kind, and caring. Thanks for all your advice and sublime Sunday roasts. Matt, it's always good to see your friendly face at Eat.St and thanks from all the traders for eating your way along the road.

And finally, the biggest thanks goes to my wonderful wife Rachel who puts food on the table when I've been too busy to eat, comforts me in times of extreme tiredness and stress, and turns out to ball when no one else can make it. Thanks for everything, with love.

Roll on.